Tell Me
Where Home Is

Carl M. Price

Isaiah 41:10
Fear thou not for I am with thee

You don't have to worry, God is with you.
Bro Carl Price

TELL ME WHERE HOME IS
Copyright © 2016 Carl M. Price

ISBN: 978-1539466840

PREFACE

This book provides a series of events and observations in my life from my perception. I have learned that darkness is not the absence of light, but an inability to see the light. In the sometimes darkened corners of my memories lit by what can be seen only through lenses able to observe light not seen by the naked eye resides a story not of survival, but of triumph.

While reading this book, it is possible you may experience discomfort, conflicting emotions or outburst of laughter. I invite you into this place with me that is my story.

CARL M. PRICE

ACKNOWLEDGMENT

How do you begin to say thank you when there are so many people who contributed to this book eventually being written. It is my hope that this is a thank you to the many professionals who work with children who have experienced trauma, in the medical professions, social work, childcare services and those families who reach out to help those in need.

Yet I must express my gratitude directly first and foremost to God and next to all the countless people who helped give me the courage and encouragement to write this book as well as proofreading and design. I want to thank my parents all of them, my family and my friends and the Shark Week at my cousin Joann's for being my light, my kids for being the best part of me. Hailey Price, no matter how old you get you will always be daddy's princess so just accept it. To my friends that I lost to cancer or leukemia, Amy, Jason, Chris, Areen, Brandon, Jimmy. Finally I would like to thank my wife Leni for her love, support and calm spirit and the many men and women who each day dedicate themselves to helping others.

CARL M. PRICE

CONTENTS

CARL M. PRICE

Chapter 1

Going Back

I will attempt to go back in my life, as far as I can remember, so that you can have a full perspective of the miraculous, sometimes lonely, wondrous and beautiful journey it has been. Many journeys in life involve great falls, however all begin with a first step. I wish to thank you and apologize for what you are about to experience in reading this book

.

I once heard that when you are going through a storm, don't stop until the storm has passed or you have passed through the storm. For me, this somehow applies to the many stories of children being ripped away from the hands of screaming mothers, while falling to the floor in protest, as the kids are carted off into foster care. Tears flood the faces of mothers and children, as the foster care invaders pillage their homes. Some stories recount how the little orphaned girl meets her new wealthy Daddy Big Bucks; and he spares no expense in making certain that she has a promising future. While this story is not an assault on foster care, it sure isn't about a little red curly haired girl, who's singing about the sun coming out tomorrow. Yes it has been a hard knocks life, but this story is not about Annie.

VCIS (Voice Case Information System) reports that the number of children in foster care rapidly increased between 1986 and 1990.

Many attribute this increase to parental drug usage. In the mid-80s, many parents in their 20s began to use drugs heavily and as a result, this may have caused an increase in the number who would go on to neglect their children. The Eighties was a period of the Regan Era, Live Aid, terrorist attacks and an all-out War on Drugs. The music of the 80's began with Smokey singing about Cruising and Michael Jackson Rocking with you. By the late 80's, Tracey Chapman was looking for a fast car to get away in and Public Enemy was screaming "Burn Hollywood Burn". Cocaine in the 80's was the "in thing" and you couldn't get any higher than getting high. Getting high to many was an elevation to a higher plain, release from one's inhibitions and an escape from the pain. That was possibly the only usage for the BS other than fertilizer.

The drug of choice in the black community was "marijuana, weed, pot or Mary Jane". Lyrics from the song Mary Jane by Rick James, describe how it was smoked by the bag loads and "when I'm feeling low, she comes as no surprise, Turns me on with her love and takes me to paradise". There were nickel bags, dime bags and even twenty dollar bags. I later learned that many agents in marijuana are more cancer causing than those found in tobacco smoke. In an article published by the "Cancer Journal for Clinicians", the Age-adjusted Cancer Incidence and Mortality Rates Among African Americans by Gender in the US from 1973 to 1999, increased for African American Males with cancer from just above 600,000 in 1983 to nearly 800,000 by 1993. An increase of nearly 33% in one decade. (http://caonline.amcancersoc.org/cgi/content/full/52/6/326/F2)

An August 2003, "Bureau of Justice", statistical analysis shows an increase in the incarceration rate of African American males, more than doubling from the late 1970s to 1991. Ronald Regan's War on Drugs from the 1980s to the mid-90s increased the number of defendants in U.S. District Courts from less than 10,000 to over 20,000. (http://bjs.ojp.usdoj.gov/content/glance/fedtyp.cfm)

It can be assumed by these numbers alone that the increase of drug usage in the African American community lead to the decrease in the mental health of those in that community and an increase in the numbers of Cancer Incidence and Mortality rates.

In 1988, Public Enemy Released the Album "<u>It Takes a Nation of Millions to Hold Us Back</u>". Were we the millions holding us back in the 80s? Public Enemy in their song, "Don't believe the Hype" said, "They claim that I'm a criminal. By now I wonder how some people never know the enemy could be their friend, guardian. Night of the living Baseheads. Check out the justice - and how they run it Sellin', smellin' Sniffin', riffin'. And brothers try to get swift an' Sell to their own, rob a home while some shrivel to bone, like comatose walkin' around."

Chapter 2

The Journey Begins

There is a house, though at the time, I would not have known what the term meant but it was a row house. See in Baltimore, MD in the 1970s, people with money lived in townhouses and well, let's just say we lived in a red brick row house with narrow windows. The street too was very narrow. I later learned the term for the narrow street was "alley".

If my memory serves me correctly, the house was located on Calendar Street between Pratt and Lombard Street. In the middle of the block was a two-story red brick house with white steps. As you enter through the front door, you can vividly see a little boy sitting on the floor in a dimly lit room watching a black and white television. There he is with this funny sailor's hat on his head trying to look like Gilligan from "Gilligan's Island". He has his funny sailor's hat tipped to the side, just to add a little coolness. If you could only picture this kid fighting off sleep, with his head swaying from side to side like a leaf on a branch being pushed by the wind. That kid is me! It's around 2 or 3 o'clock in the afternoon and that means it's coming up on naptime. I must have been about age 3.

"Carl", a voice calls from the kitchen that smells like collard greens and cornbread with a mixture of fried chicken and my favorite, macaroni and cheese. The smells that would escape the kitchen each afternoon were intoxicating to the mind of a young child. There is something about the smell of cakes, pies and sugar being baked that to a child it's like the beautiful sweet scent of perfume worn by an exotic woman to a lonely sailor. There were other scents of chicken, breads and sounds of Diana Ross, the Commodores and Donna Summer. I can still hear the laughter of my grandmother, as she danced around the house, keeping the temperature of the wood burning in the oven just right, while making time to clean the house, play with me and still dance and laugh.

It has been nearly 40 years and I still have never met anyone nearly as beautiful as my grandmother. The only one that comes close is my daughter when she's smiling and laughing at me. "Poo Poo" as my grandmother affectionately called me over the sound of the TV and the music coming from the kitchen. Back then and even now, I hate when anyone calls me that name. But when my grandmother called me "Poo Poo", it was like music to my ears and a call from heaven, passing through the clouds and gently presenting itself to humanity. "I see you in there" said my grandmother. I smiled while turning my head towards the kitchen, but not my eyes so that I would not miss a single second of what was on T.V. "I gotta stay awake", I thought rubbing my little eyes. I could hear heavy footsteps heading in my direction from the kitchen. The kitchen was emitting so much heat that it felt like the sun was having a cup of tea at the kitchen table. "Come on hang in there," I thought, as I stretched and tried to keep my eyes open, while rubbing them, as if to shake them awake. Her long legs seemed to just appear suddenly. "No Moma".

It is important that we stop here to explain how the name "Moma" is pronounced. It is not Momma but MO Muh. I believe someone had trouble pronouncing Momma and Moma stuck.

"No Moma, I'm not sleepy yet" cried the little boy as she lifted him up to what seemed like miles into the air. The tall beautiful black woman, had long pretty black hair and eyes that seemed to have magic inside of them. Before the little boy made it to her shoulder he had fallen asleep, but I still remember hearing her giggle and saying "I know baby I know." I recall the times when she picked me up in her arms, the motion was always slow and careful, as if she was handling a very delicate package. When I needed her she was always there for me; and when I talked, she listened. I never got away with much, but her discipline was always focused on getting me to understand that what I did was wrong and should not be done again. Respect was mandatory in her home and no child was ever allowed to forget it. When speaking with an adult, you were expected to show respect and respond by saying "mam or sir". Her house was a home and in that home I had many great adventures. One such adventure can be described as a moment of innocence gone bad. It all began with a spoon and a jar of peanut butter, this by itself seems simple enough so, you need only add a little mischief. My grandmother left the kitchen for only a short time, providing me with the perfect opportunity to have a meeting with mischief. I carefully slid the wooden drawer open slowly, trying not to make a sound or have the utensils hitting against one another, while looking over my shoulder at the same time with the fear of being caught. With the spoon in hand, I climbed up onto the chair with the silence of a well-trained ninja to reach the counter and get the jar of peanut butter. To save time, I decided to take just one spoonful of peanut butter rather than going back and forth multiple times. I quickly stuffed the spoonful of peanut butter into my mouth. If you are laughing already this can only mean that you too may have done this or witnessed it happening. The peanut butter and spoon acted like an adhesive to the roof of my mouth, and to make matters worse, it was at that moment, that very moment that my grandmother returns to the kitchen. Feeling ashamed and not wanting to make eye contact, I simply looked down at the floor. As I looked up, I could see the smile on her face and hear her giggle as she shook her head, while opening the refrigerator to pour me a glass of milk. There was so much mischief to get into at my grandmother's house and as a child, I made every attempt to regular meetings with mischief.

One such regularly scheduled meeting with mischief was when I wanted to go to the playground nearby, but everyone was too busy to take me. There was a street that had to be crossed to get to the playground and the simple two lane street seemed more like a grand canyon of an obstacle that day, at least until mischief began whispering again. Perhaps it was just me, but whenever mischief wanted to do something that would later get me in trouble, it always seemed to whisper so no one would know whose idea it was. I quietly made my way to the door, making no eye contact with anyone to prevent drawing any attention. I remember thinking if I don't look back I won't see anyone so no one will see me. Keep your eyes on the prize and the prize was that metal sliding board at the playground which I loved to go down. I got to the corner and before I could talk myself out of it mischief said, hurry it's waiting for you. I ran across the street and made it to the playground. The slide that day seemed extra slippery and I seemed to come down it faster than ever. There were no lines so I could go down as many times as I wanted and then, you know there had to be a then moment. As I can down the slide, out of focus in the distance across the street I could see a shape, it was an adult and I was hoping it was my Aunt Carolyn or Cynthia because they seemed to understand that it was mischief's idea when I got in trouble more than the others. It was Moma.

I walked to the corner and waited for her to tell me it was safe for me to cross the street, but she didn't say a word and the goofy smile I had on my face wasn't helping. Eventually she called for me to cross the street and as I walked up to her she reached down and hugged me tightly. "Never ever leave the house like that again." She seemed more afraid than I was and as she held my hand we walked home. "Moma you should've seen me I was going fast." We laughed and went back into the house.

At that point in my life, I can't say that I knew or even understood the meaning of pain. Also, I can't say that I had any hatred in my heart towards anyone and if you had asked me what I thought about the world, which at that time was only about the size of

West Baltimore, I probably would have said, "it's a pretty cool place". Funny thing is that, I don't think I was even aware that I was black or any different from the white kids at the playground, except maybe they were lighter because they didn't get to play in the sun too much.

As a child, the red bricked row house on Calendar St in West Baltimore was a castle to me and I was its prince. I never realized at the time that we were poor, in fact I thought we were rich. So much love and laughter filled the house that it seemed to be pouring out the windows, if this wasn't rich then what else could rich be?

Later in life, I described my grandmother's love, as the greatest love I have ever known. She was so beautiful with her dark brown skin, almost the same color as mine, unlike Sam my uncle or Miley, Wendy and Ann my aunts. Walter my other uncle was also about my complexion and so was Arlethia, Carolyn, Cynthia and the lady who looked so much like Moma and came by to visit from time to time. She was pretty too. Just wish she wouldn't be hugging up on me so much whenever she came to visit. They called her Rose or Rosie. A rose by any other name? We'll deal with that one a little later.

I remember one day perhaps a few months or weeks later that the woman they called Rose or Rosie came to the house and whatever she said to Moma didn't make her too happy because they were yelling at each other. Often people in our house would get loud with laughter and excitement, like when Cynthia was talking about how fine this brother walking down the street had been. Cynt as she was affectionately called was the youngest in the house next to me. She always made time to check on me. Sam was tall and smooth. He had a way of walking yet leaning at the same time and not falling. I remember this because I recall trying it and I fell over. Miley was tall and pretty like the ladies I used to see in magazines. She had what I remember thinking was sleepy eyes. For those of you who may not understand the sleepy eyes you will a little later. Wendy and Walter were twins, yet as different as night and day. Wendy had a huge smile and it seemed she never stopped smiling. She seemed to find peace with the world as it was, while Walter was a rebel without a cause. He was looking for some purpose and questioned everything. The funny thing about Walter was that to the outside world he may have seemed like some foolish idiot, but he was the first man I ever remember hearing say that he loved me. He would say "remember Uncle Walter loves you, but you don't have to put up with no shit from anybody". When I think about him now, the Public enemy song, "Fight the Power" rings in my head. Arlethia, I don't recall much except scattered memories. Carolyn was another aunt yet she was so much more. The way the story was explained to me is that her birthday was March 4th and because I wasn't scheduled to be born yet my mother was with her celebrating her birthday when I heard the music and wanted to see what was going on. So a little after midnight on March 5th I arrived into the world. I don't know if it was because of how I arrived or some other reason but Carolyn and I would always be close. Ann was quiet even in this busy house, but when she smiled, it was like she had accomplished something or like the cat that had quietly eaten the pet bird and still no one had discovered it was missing. I always wondered about her because we never became close. Ann once insisted that I let her put a relaxer like Michael Jackson's in my hair. After a while, I began to explain to her that my head was getting hot. She brushed me off by saying "it's okay". Moments later, I remember running through the house screaming, "It's hot, it's hot!" as the relaxer did all but relax me. I don't remember who grabbed me and rinsed it out, but I didn't let a woman touch my hair again for many years. When I heard the story of Sampson and Delilah and how a woman took him out by messing with his hair, I recall thinking yeah brother I feel your pain. Finally there was Rosia or Rosie as they called her. She seemed to somehow have a mixture of all the others. When she would smile it was contagious. She was tall and pretty but seemed like the type you didn't want to upset because when she was not smiling her look could silence a room. She didn't live in the house but came by from time to time.

With this many people in and out of the house the loudness would normally quickly stop once Moma gave that certain look. You know the look, the look mothers used to give that though not a single word was said would communicate to all nearby and even those in other rooms that seemed to say, Ok enough. Even I knew at that early point of my life that this look meant calm down, however the yelling didn't seem to stop this time when Rosie came. I can't recall, if it was night or day time, but the room was dimly lit and Harold Moma's boyfriend, my best friend at the time held me in his big strong arms daring anyone to as much as reach for me. Now Harold was very dark. He was so dark Moma called him Smokey and King Kong to make him mad, but that just seemed to tickle Harold because he would always whisper to me, "she just mad cus she aint as dark as me" and I would laugh and ask if I would someday be able to be as dark. He would always reply, "You gotta work to be this handsome son." I don't recall a man calling me son again for more than 11 years. There I was though, in Harold's big strong arms trying to hear the television over the screaming when for some reason, which I didn't understand, nor cared to understand, Harold handed me to that woman. I recall feeling fear enter my heart. To a child fear can be all consuming; it can cause your muscles to lock in place and a chilling pain to run up your spine and sometimes cause the muscles to rapidly pulsate. This may be why when children are yelled at or feel fear the first reaction is to stand motionless or scream. I remember wanting to scream when she grabbed my arm and pulled me away from my safe place, but I was so scared that the words would not come out. Fear had taken such a hold on me that the natural reflex to scream for help sat dormant, perhaps itself too afraid to make a sound. The look in my eyes surely was screaming louder than any cry I could have made, however no assistance was provided.

With confusion and panic in my eyes, I looked at Moma as if to say, "I am sorry, I'll go to bed now" while stretching my arms out pleading for her to take me. With her beautiful eyes stirring back at me, I could see the black in the center as dark as coal, surrounded by an ocean of brown and from these almond shaped eyes came tears flowing like a river pouring down her face. I could see the magic that once filled her eyes being replaced by pain. Traumatized by what was happening, I asked myself, " Did I do something wrong?", "What did I break now?" Still confused, I thought, "It can't be that piece of cake Wendy and I had eaten the day before and never told anyone?" As a child undergoing trauma I dared to asses why this was happening. A few minutes seemed blurry but before I knew anything, this woman had taken me out into the street and put me into the back seat of a car. I began yelling while gazing at Harold, my best friend and super hero, pleading for him to save me; defeat this evil villain and restore peace, but he stood there with those huge arms unable to come to my aid. Superman had his kryptonite, but what could have been so strong that could have kept him from coming to rescue me? "Moma" I yelled out "Moma", then the car, a blue Cadillac pulled off with me inside.

Traveling down streets I had never seen before pass places I had never been or known existed, we arrived at some strange house I had never visited. No one carried me out of the car or into the house in their arms like I had been accustomed to being treated. Harold used to carry me everywhere but this woman and man that I had never before seen had problems treating me the same way. Once in the house hey tried to get me to lie down on some bed, but I resisted. Resistance would later become far more a common assurance. Popping up each time that she pushed me back down. "No! Lay down Montes." What did she call me? There was no one else in the room and she was looking directly at me. "No I wanna". "Time for bed Montes." Who is she talking to? Then with a commanding tone that would force the greatest army to obey she said, "Carl Montes Price, if you don't get in this bed." I had never been called that name before but was that my name? I looked at this woman and for a split second, it was like Moma was looking back at me, so I began to lay back until the light from the open door came across her face. This is where it all began, like a great ship casting off to some great destination or possibly heading into some incredible storm, it began with the words from this little boy in his little sweet innocent voice. Words formed from an innocent mind, shaped from a small world that he was about to leave forever and never return, "I wanna go home."

Have you ever recalled a time in your life that reminded you of a dramatic scene in a movie? Well, this would have been the scene when silence fell upon the room and a single spotlight was cast upon the boy crying out, "I Wanna Go Home". These words seemed to race through the room and out the door. I wanted so badly for my cry for help to reach the place that was so familiar to me...home. This scene in the movie had the spotlight shining and waiting for Batman to come, but no hero would rush to my aid. My cry for help would go unanswered.

When is it that a boy begins to become a man? Some would say that it begins in the teen years. Looking back, I can recall that the little boy and I began to go our separate ways there in that moment. The little sweet voice of a child starts to lose its innocence and the voice of a man is being revealed. Innocence, simplicity; absence of guile or cunning, I don't know, but I would never again be that little boy. I would forever hold onto the little boy's dreams; try to heal his scars and somehow, some way, some day, answer his call for help.

Chapter 3

The Introduction

By the time you get to the last chapter in this book, it is my hope that you will understand how profound those words would later become that poured from the mouth of such innocence. An innocence that once left, would never be revisited again. "I WANNA GO HOMMMMME." A voice demanding its return to its rightful place. A voice not unlike those of its ancestors crying in their native tongue to be returned to their mother land so many years before, not so different from the argument of men asking for their rights that they were born with.

Do you recall your first memory of your mother? Not your first meeting but your first memory of her. Possibly playing together, baking some desert in the kitchen or laughing in the park. Do you recall the face of a woman smiling at you and possibly laughing with you? Perhaps a memory that is just so happy, you are smiling now recalling the moment. Well my memory goes a little like this. There is this dark room with very little light, so there are large dark shadows running across the walls and in that room it is very cold so those shadows seem to bring a chill with their approach. There are no pictures on the walls and there she sat at the side of the bed, this woman whom I hadn't a clue who she was and the conversation continues, "I WANNA GOOOO HOMMMMME, I want my Moma" now demanding the little voice once so soft and polite. Remember the silence that fell upon the room well the silence was interrupted by her hand slapping me across the left side of my face. It could have been the sound of a cannon firing at an enemy or that of a missile striking its target. You don't know which to fear more the impact or the sound. After all, is it the thunder or the lightning that causes most people to jump in fear? "I am your mother and you are home" the thunder echoed across the sky accompanied only by the silence that would follow.

Before that moment, I can never remember anything more than a light spanking on my bottom. So fear and I had our first introduction this day. As if to establish roles, fear quickly introduced his partners shock and pain. If there was going to be an Alpha male in this new relationship, fear was certainly putting in for the job. My face felt something it had never felt before and I was so frightened that I couldn't even cry. Do you know what the definition of fear truly is? Well let me tell you my thought. Fear is a feeling of agitation and anxiety caused by the presence of imminent danger. DANGER! Please watch your step because up ahead there will be imminent danger. You know like a baby at some point learns not to crawl too close to the edge of the bed, or a child learns someday not to put his hand too close to the fire. I too learned at that moment, you do not play with fire! (There is a later point at which I feel I leave never to return but there are some who will read this and feel I never really arrived here.) ?????

They called her Rosie, although her name was spelled Rosia. Perhaps a nickname you would think, but she later told me the "a" in Rosia was silent. You'll understand that one later perhaps. Rosia Lee Price, daughter to Miley Glover (Moma) and Sam Price Sr. She was tall and very pretty. She had hair like Moma, eyes like Moma and she was slender like her with the same complexion. Her Friend was an older man who seemed closer to Harold's age more so than her own. They called him Hamm. He was David Hamm and he was as cold as that dark room on my first night with them. The other very noticeable distinction about Hamm was that he was nowhere near the complexion of Harold. He was a rather light skinned man, who had a cold lifeless reflection in his eyes.

His stare seemed as if it would reach in and chill your very soul.

In Shakespeare's Romeo and Juliet, Juliet tells Romeo that a name is artificial and meaningless. "What's in a name? That which we call a rose by any other name would smell as sweet." Over the years, I have purchased dozens of roses for many different occasions and each time I attempted to smell them only to find myself caught in its thorns. A rose is a beautiful flower sitting atop a long thin stem surrounded by thorns to protect it but harming any who come too close. This flower seemed to describe her so well, after all a Rose by any other name would smell just as sweet, right?

The sun eventually rose, now that's where I later found my salvation in the rising of the sun and I looked out upon this new world and saw that I was in trouble. It was not some crazy nightmare, I was awake and now sitting up in this unfamiliar place missing Moma and Harold wondering would they ever come for me or if they even knew where I was. The door was partially closed and the sun was reaching through the window while I was drying the tears on my face. When you're afraid you tend to move as quietly as possible, so not to draw any attention by revealing your position. So I sat there quiet and motionless as fear set up a parameter around me. Now cowering in the corner of the bed like a prisoner awakened in his cell, I was too afraid to even breathe in too much oxygen for fear of further punishment. I heard movement outside the door and hoped that if I did not make any noise, they would not enter the room.

Prior to this time, I was used to waking up to soft sounds, whispers like "don't wake him up" or the smell of breakfast cooking. Sometimes someone would literally come pick me up out of bed and carry me down to the table to eat, but this day was unlike any I had ever experienced. I grew up thinking my grandmother was my mother. She was angelic, with an even brown complexion and as I remember she always had her hair down. When my grandmother smiled, it was like being tickled by an angel. It was only after this very traumatic experience that I realized Moma was not my mother. The definition of the word trauma means an experience that produces psychological injury or pain. Although not yet in my vocabulary, the definition of the word trauma and its impact I would soon experience. The injuries from trauma, if not properly reset or cared for can be like a broken bone left untreated which can lead to a permanent disorder. I feel the need to say that again, the injuries from trauma, if not properly reset or cared for can be like a broken bone left untreated which can lead to a permanent disorder. Pain is the body's way of alerting the brain that something is wrong. With psychological trauma the emotional pain and despair one feels afterwards, can be such an alert to the brain.

Seized by the unknown and fear, I watched the door and listened to every sound. I focused on the door so much that with my eyes, I poured over the hinges with residue of rust seeping out from the paint and noticed the cracked paint barely able to hold itself to the door. A silent house will scream and moan if there is nothing else to hear and there is an active ear participating.

It took me nearly 30 years, but I finally found that house in the 2700 block of Rosalind Ave. In looking back, I asked myself "Why doesn't this dummy get up and run?" In a scary movie, the person is so gripped by fear that they are unable to move. I would later study the concept of Flee, Fight or Freeze, where the freeze response comes when there is an assumption that there is no hope of surviving. For years I had a returning nightmare that I was killed at this home and in each dream I was never able to run away. Though dreaming of being killed is very frightening, dreaming that it was your mother intentionally killing you as you leave the house seems to address not only the fear but the possibility of punishment for any attempt of leaving. There would be no attempt to cross the street without permission here.

There was a big rock or boulder outside of the house and I can remember playing on it. As we grow up, things that once seemed like mountains become simple bumps along the way. These mountains are not always physical obstacles. Often, people will stop at the foot of such obstacles and never attempt to go any further or simply turn back rather than face the obstacles. In my dreams, it was my mother that would kill me each time violently.

One night I was having a nightmare and I couldn't wake up from it. I was breathing hard and rolling around. The dream would not end and suddenly I felt a soft hand touching me as if pulling me from the dream. When I opened my eyes I thought I was seeing Moma. As I smiled, my eyes began to focus and I could see it was my mother instead of Moma. She had tears in her eyes and I suddenly felt the need to protect her. My mother was just 15 when she gave birth to me and she was the first of her siblings to give birth. So my grandmother raised me, as so many others did during that time.

It didn't take long before my mother and I became friends after that night. We would joke around and laugh till tears fell from our eyes. She would laugh as I pretended to walk like Sam, leaning to the side with a little bop in each step. He was tall and as cool as a winter night. His way of walking yet leaning at the same time and not falling was the very essence of cool. It's funny they call that swagger now. My mother became nearly as wonderful as Moma for short periods of time or until "he" would return home. It was as if, his presence triggered a different side of her. She would become distant and disconnected once he arrived. By observing women later in my life, I realized that sometimes, women will attempt to make a man feel important by removing all attention from the children and placing it exclusively on the man. Some women perhaps believed that this gave them more security by catering to the man's needs and making them feel important.

Children desire attention and approval and when there is a lack of such the child often acts out. When Hamm would act out there would be arguments filled with threats and yelling and fighting. In the midst of one such argument, Hamm looked at me with cold eyes as a hunter focuses on its prey and said, "The only reason you got him was for that welfare check." His words no longer had the sting to get a reaction from my mother, so he turned to me. What was intended to dent her armor would leave a crater in mine which would remain for decades. I was nothing more to her than a means to get a check, I thought. His attack that day caused me to question my own self-worth. I had begun to think that my mother had come to get me because she missed and loved me and wanted me with her.

Often the things that are said to a child can be just as damaging as the things done to a child. Mental trauma many times leaves the same impairment as physical. Telling a child they are stupid, calling him or her out of their name, blaming children and many other verbal assaults can be like shooting shotgun shells at the child's brain development. Children who are bullies can sometimes be found being mentally bullied themselves in their homes and a male child's need for acceptance by the immediate males in his life can lead to shaping his perception of the world.

Chapter 4

In the Event of an Emergency

When children enter school, they are required to take home an Emergency Contact Card. At that time or in the 1970's, this is what they had us do in Baltimore City Public Schools. It was nothing more than a 3" x 5" index card with questions like Mother's Name, address, phone number, Father's Name, address, phone number. There was also a line that read, "In the event of an Emergency contact," with check boxes next to the mother's and father's information. I remember getting my card like everyone else and skipping home. I would take my time walking through Cross Street Market smelling the hundreds of scents from the raw meats to the fresh baked goods, even the flowers and tobacco would tickle my senses, but none more than the smell of the fresh potato chips at the Utz vendor, who would sometimes give me a free sample of what was left and not sold that day.

Baltimore in the late 70s was very diverse in its mixture of citizens. Cross Street Market seemed to house all of these cultures in one long stretched out community. There were the German influences like the hot dogs with sauerkraut, the entire market would be Irish Green for St. Patrick's Day, the Asian lady always sold her Made in China goods from sunglasses to hats to watches and though no black person seemed to own a single stand, there were plenty working there. There was chocolate and fresh fish, Chinese food and fried chicken, but there was always some adult from the neighborhood who knew who you were so you knew not to run through the market or do anything that could get you in trouble. No running, pushing or being disrespectful and when an elder walked near you it was you who got out of their way. This was an unspoken but very clearly understood set of rules for us in Cross Street Market back then.

I got home with my Emergency Contact Card that day and because I could read and write I decided to fill the card out myself, at least what information I could. I completed the entire side without any help with my mother's information. I had even learned what our zip code was from the Ebony magazines that would come in the mail each month. When it was time to complete the side with my father's information I went to my mother's room where she was lying on the bed watching TV. She smiled when I walked into the room and said, "Hey baby what are you doing?" I showed her how I had completed her side of the card. I was very proud of what I was able to do, but when she saw what was not completed her smile immediately left and was replaced by a look that I had come to fear. It was that look that always came just before the storm, as if the dark clouds came rolling in or that look of imminent danger. She handed me the card back and turned back towards the television. I explained to her that I needed my father's information so that I could complete the card and have it back to school on time the next day. Her response though not the first time I had ever had something taken from me, was devastating. "You don't have a father." It was like she walked into the fabric of my existence and removed a part of what made me. Somehow she felt she could expel 50% of my existence, remove my blood lineage or just erase the remaining memories I had of my father. How could I not have a father?

"But the teacher said that we had to fill this out completely before we take it back", I explained to her. "Well you tell your teacher I'm your father." "But mom!" The space there represents the silence after she hit me and I laid there motionless for fear of a continued assault. You ever notice how quiet it is right after you hear thunder during a storm? It's almost as if everything is waiting to see what happens next. I couldn't even look at her. I took the card and left the room. I didn't look back and I refused to even shed a tear in her presence. I did not want her to know how much this had hurt me, the removal of my father or the pain from being hit. I was not willing to allow her to feel any accomplishment by showing her I was hurt.

The next day when the teacher asked for our cards, I waited for a crowd to gather then I rushed into the crowd and dropped my card on her desk, hoping that she would not have time to give my card enough attention to notice the blank side. I immediately rushed back to my seat. She began to call names out and as she called each name she said what was missing from the cards, then explained to each child that they would have to take the card home and bring it back completed. "Carl M. Price." When she called my name I wanted to run out of the room before she could announce to the entire class that my father's information was not there. I wouldn't make any eye contact. You know, no sudden moves and I looked straight down at the desk. I never noticed before just how much writing was on my desk. Chris N Shawn 2gether 4ever. Mark got a big head scribbled in ink on the desk. Someone had even tried to draw a three dimensional, Carl M. Price, she called again, this time even louder. Huh? Is huh some automatic response when we wish to pretend to either not hear or understand the statement or question that preceded it? I wanted her to correct me for saying huh, but when you want them to do something, it is just then that they won't. "Carl did you give these cards to your mother?" Yes Mam I did. "Get up here and fill out your father's information." "WHAT." I said it with as much attitude as I could so I could and finally did get results. You see if there was anything that was going to get me out of this, it was going to require me taking control of the situation and causing the teacher to throw me out of the class to give me time. Time for what I don't know, perhaps I would see my Aunt Barbara my father's sister and she could give me his information. I just didn't want the entire class knowing I didn't have my father's information.

CARL M. PRICE

Many would think that the teacher had control, but she was on the hook now because I triggered her ego. See a child that young should have known nothing about what I later began to term responsive behavior. What this is, is you create an action with the full purpose of causing a set reaction. Later in life when reading the Art of War, I discovered this was an important form of knowing your enemy. I needed to get out of the class. I didn't know any more about my father other than his name was Eddie and he was in jail and I remember how he used to smile at me like I was valuable to him. How was I to place that on an Emergency Contact card? Like if some emergency were to take place, they would call the jail ask for him and they would walk him to the phone to take the call and send someone for me. Sometimes I wished that I could just call him even if it wasn't an emergency just so I could hear his deep voice and his strong laughter.

The teacher became angry by how I responded to her and as expected and needed she kicked me out of class. "Get out of my class and go down to the office." As I walked out of the class room I made a point to slam the door to make certain she wasn't about to have second thoughts about sending me out of her class and as if counting in my head I walked slowly waiting to see just how long before, 1, 2, 3 there it is. The door swung open and she came busting out. As I turned to face her I could see that somehow my plan didn't go quite as well as expected. "Get your behine (something adults would say to kids back in the day. If it were your mother it would have been get your black ass) back in that class boy and I don't want to have to hear your mouth again." The first thought I had was, note to self the slamming door may have been the wrong response. Try something different. As I sat down and the kids were laughing, not laughing at me but laughing that I was brave enough to even try that stunt, it hit me when I looked up at her, she knew why I did the whole thing. It may have taken her a moment but she knew. I could tell that she knew because when she looked back at me, it wasn't a look of anger but more so a look of empathy. I never had to get the card completed that year and we never talked about it. There were plenty of black boys who didn't have fathers around in that neighborhood, so I guess it wasn't as rare an incident as I thought at the time. Still I felt safe for that moment in that classroom. I would have to say that this incident was one of the greatest of the countless incidents that lead to me becoming the man that I am now today by having a severe impact on my attitude towards hearing what people don't say when they are talking.

School and more the pursuit of understanding via knowledge became an immediate safeguard for me. The math and science classes were often the only assurances I had because of their exact answers. So in these classes, I dominated without exclusion. Many of the kids in my classes were facing the same instabilities at home that I faced but were unable to find shelter and would often fall behind in class, too afflicted by the hungry stomachs, broken homes, alcohol, drugs and lack of resources. Lower grades triggered fighting and the loss of interest in participating. This was not helped by the statistical evidence often quoted to us by teachers with the intent to motivate us, but like that of haunting sounds or Taps played by a lone soldier at a funeral, it seemed to merely announce the pending eventual damning end that we would have to face. Statistically, black males were more likely to end up dead or in jail, than make it out of the ghetto by the time they were 25. These announcements of the statistics were intended to be an alarm to awaken the minds of our fragile lives. I recently read that although Blacks in America may no longer be the largest minority, we make up nearly 50% of the prison population (Bureau of Justice Statistics 2005). The sirens rang out loud from teachers crying, pleading and laying all they had on the line to save a generation. As the school bell rang at the end of each day, was it a bell signaling far more than simply the end of class? The red box with its white handle hanging on the wall in each classroom for emergencies, had no counterpart in the realities that faced so many kids as they exited the doors of the schools returning to the real world that created those statistics.

One of the most powerful unifiers I have identified in my life is hunger, physical hunger to be exact. The wide range in differences between the homes we live in, cars we drive, even ways in which we clothe our bodies so quickly separate us, yet when hunger arrives a common instinct triggers, a need to feed that hunger. A man or woman living in a home with a pantry and refrigerator full of food would in most cases never consider eating food from a trash can, but take the same man, remove all the food, remove the home and strangle his hope, suddenly the possibility of eating from the trash can becomes more considerable.

Though Baltimore had its invisible race lines many of the poor whites were housed near the poor blacks speaking a common language of despair. The free school lunch program for many was the only balanced or guaranteed nutrition that many poor kids had and watching how some kids ate was evidence of the importance of these meals. Some kids routinely placing parts of their lunch in their pockets so they may have something to eat when they get home.

By this point I knew with certainty that we were poor. Perhaps the holes in the bottom of my shoes, the clothes that were purchased from the thrift stores or the sounds my stomach would make sometimes in class signaled to me that we were poor and there was no laughter to fill the empty stomachs with hope just occasional help from different aunts. Linda another one of my father's sisters would ask whenever I visited her, "You want something to eat?" I don't know if it was because I was such a poor sight to see or she just knew I needed it.

Chapter 5

.

Beauty

There is nothing beautiful about a naked canvas. It cannot be what it is designed to be until it does what it is called to do. It must be painted to find who it truly is. The same can be said for the mind of a child. It is bare and cannot be what it has been designed to be, until it has been painted. Painted with history and calculations, facts, fictions, new thoughts and restrictions. These are the colors that paint the canvas of a child's mind. I had a teacher who had the ability to paint wondrous beauty in my mind. She was an Elementary School teacher and her name was Ms. Thompson. It was in her explanation of math that I finally found my place of peace. She had the attitude and taught certain students that to be able to one day compete with the white students, who had both mothers and fathers in their homes, who had scholarships already set up for them and statistics in their favor, we would have to work twice as hard to not only combat the issues of race but those of poverty as well. Ms. Thompson was at Federal Hill Elementary School, located minutes from Federal Hill Park and Baltimore's famous Inner Harbor.

RACE

During the late 70's and early 80's, like South Baltimore's population the school was cluttered with many different cultures and ethnicities. There were poor blacks, poor whites, a few newly American immigrants and some whites, who saw what was happening with downtown and moved near and around the Federal Hill area to take advantage of the city's growth. These were whites, who had money and their children seemed to have it all. There was this kid whose name was David. His best friend was Noah and the two of them appeared to have it all. Although David's parents were divorced, (this is the first time in my life I had ever heard that word and it took many years before I truly understood what it meant) he had it made. One week he stayed with his dad and the next week he was with his mom. They would compete for the title Best Parent. I wonder how hard it must have been for David. I wonder which place he called home. The struggle they he may have faced and the trauma being torn between two homes and was his trauma possibly ignored because the material things that surrounded him is a question I now look back and wonder.

I lived in a little small house that had a first floor not much bigger than the office I presently have today. There was the living room and then the kitchen, between the two was the very narrow staircase that went upstairs which had two bedrooms and a bathroom so small that if the water in the sink ran over it spilled in either the toilet or the bath tub. The house was so bad that it was condemned after we moved away many years later. When you entered the house there was a hole in the floor and you could see straight down to the ground below the foundation. I believe the landlord was never called to repair it because my mother's boyfriend Hamm dropped some part of a truck's transmission on the floor one night when he was bringing it into the house to work on. I do not recall what the part was but the grease and oil covered metal was hard to hold onto and when it hit the floor it didn't even slow down to notice that the floor was even there. The home had only two heaters. I remember this because on very cold winter nights I remember asking if I could sleep at the foot of my mother and her boyfriend's bed to keep warm because the heaters were in their bedroom and the living room. The address was 111 W. West

TELL ME WHERE HOME IS

Street Baltimore, MD 21230. There was a bus company across the street and as kids, we would explore the empty buses on Sundays when the mechanics were off work. Hide and go seek was the game of choice then for us. Between the many buses and parked cars on the streets, you had to be able to run fast to find anyone. Though I cannot remember the name of the bus company, I remember the buses were charter buses and they were red and white. The seats were red and another color and sometimes you could find change lost by former passengers between the seats. Sometimes when I hid on the buses, I would sit in the seats and imagine I was going someplace like D.C., New York or even California, just anyplace except Baltimore. Sometimes I would sit, close my eyes and imagine what it was like in other places. I would imagine the mountains or the dessert or even seeing the ocean, but that all seemed so far away.

For everyone not from Baltimore who may find themselves reading this, the word is pronounced Baldimore. If you have ever heard anyone from Baltimore, black, white, rich or poor, it's just how we say it. Consider it being like Maryland Crab cakes, you have to have Old Bay Seasoning or it's just not right, same with how we pronounce our city, Baldimore. Ok now that's out of the way let us continue.

My hair style was in an afro, bush or whatever you prefer to call it depending on where you were from during that time. I preferred to call it a mess. For those who have or had one, remember with me if you can, a pick or comb. The significance here is that a pick is stronger than a comb, thicker than most combs and designed to pull the hair. Now imagine taking this pick pulling on hair that could be compared to wool. My hair was NAPPY! In the streets of Baltimore and across this vast country in the many communities occupied by African American citizens, we tend to call that NAPPY. This is why you must use a pick to get the hair to cooperate. It can be a very painful process picking hair like wool. Both for the person whose head feels like the hair is being pulled out of their head and for the person who is picking's wrist.

So here I was the little black boy with a big bush and for some reason there was this little blonde hair white girl who seemed to like me and called herself my girlfriend. I don't recall too much about Paula or how she looked but I do remember her father and her brother who was maybe a year older than us at the time and they both chewed tobacco and she had done it too sometimes. I would walk her home from elementary school sometimes because it wasn't out of my way and to watch her father spit the tar like tobacco from his mouth into the gutter like it was target practice for him. She lived above Hanover Street which then housed a vast majority of the whites who lived in South Baltimore. One day after walking her home and convincing her father that my mother would literally kill me if she even thought I was chewing tobacco, while walking down her street I saw something written in chalk on the dark asphalt street. Paula is a Nigger lover. I didn't truly understand what I was reading at the time. I did understand that Nigger was a term used by white people towards black people but that was about it. When I got home I explained to my dark complexion, tall slender black mother what I had seen. She sat me down and looked into my eyes with a look as if to say to me what I am about to explain to you is going to hurt. We were in the kitchen and I can remember the white and yellow walls. She began explaining by asking me to look at my hand. This is the same hand I had been using for the last 6 to 7 years now and so I wasn't sure what it was she was hoping I would find. She asked me to look at its shape, to count the fingers and tell her what I saw. By this age I understood that my mother sometimes would get strange because of her drug usage or abuse of alcohol, so I just played along. Five fingers and a hand, I replied. She then opened a magazine and found a picture of a white man holding a glass. She asked me to look at his hand, its shape and to count the fingers. His hand is like my hand with 5 fingers I said. Now what difference do you see other than the size of your two hands? Still thinking this line of questioning was odd, I played along to see how far out she would go. Well my hand is darker because I am brown and he looks yellow but that's all. The look on her face almost appeared like a great weight was now placed upon her. It was as if someone had come into the room and placed some great societal burden or assignment on her and she knew what it would mean after this point to continue. Up to this point you see, to the true differences in color and race I was still naked like Adam before eating of the tree of knowledge. This knowledge like Adam's would cause my eyes to open and I would be able to see evil. "Montes", this is a name I only allow a select group to call me because whenever my mother called me by that name it was to comfort or encourage me. "Montes, baby you know you are black right." "Yes", I replied. "Well because you are black some people don't see that as being your only difference. They see that difference causing many other differences. Some think they are better than you just because you are black." My mother went on to explain to me how black men were treated differently just because they were black men, how blacks had to deal with segregation, Jim Crow and slavery. She pointed to the stack of Ebony magazines on the table and explained how many cannot see the beauty in our color they just see the difference and that clouds their judgment. "Montes, you are going to someday be one of those black men and people will look at you and see only the black and not the man. Some will hate not who you are but what you are, but you must know this no matter what you hear, you are beautiful, but it is not your black that makes you beautiful, it's you."

Interrupting the pride I was feeling, was the fear that entered my heart. I recalled the pictures of Emmett Till I had seen in an issue of Ebony or Jet Magazine. The pictures were very vivid. I remember when I was flipping through the pages and saw the image I dropped the magazine and my mother turning and looking at me with an upset look on her face until she saw the open page and the fear in my eyes. With her right hand she touched the side of my face and with the other she closed the magazine saying only, "What are you doing looking in this magazine, did it scare you baby." I asked her what happened to that boy in the picture and when she told me I felt so cold like a chill had entered not only the room but me. So here again this fear had returned bigger and badder than before. This little black boy was killed for speaking to a white girl. With the image of his disfigured face locked in my head I began to now see the writing on the asphalt from before "NIGGER". The person they were talking about was me. I began to wonder if what happened to Emmitt was about to happen to me. The next day when I went to school I made a very conscious effort not to sit near or speak to Paula. I could tell she was hurt by my actions but in the mind of a 6 or 7 year old I had to do whatever I could to not trigger the same course of events that lead to the demise of Emmett Till. I would like to tell you that after a day or so the fear was gone and Paula and I went back to being good friends but I can't because that never happened. We never really talked again. Each time I walked home and was above Hanover Street I was always very careful to notice who was around me and refused to ever show any fear. I said to myself that if anyone came for me, I would do all that I could to protect myself no matter what it took, even if that was to mean losing a friend. Paula and I saw each other many years later as adults. We said perhaps 10 words to each other and never saw each other again.

This would not be the only racially charged experience I would have growing up in Baltimore City. I had a friends named Willie, I do not know if his name was William and we called him Willie as a nickname or if his name was just Willie but I only ever knew him as Willie. Willie had a little brother and we were all quite young in elementary school. They lived on Hanover Street near where the invisible racial divide was. They lived so close that when you looked you of the back window of their house all you could see in the summer were white people.

Willie's house was near the corner of Hanover and Montgomery Streets and we would run between Montgomery and Hughes Streets laughing for hours and sometimes go to the store to get candy then run even more. It would not be rude to say that sometimes we may have gotten a little too loud, I know this because Willie's mother once said we were making so much noise we were about to wake up the dead. I wasn't a scaredy cat, but I had no interest in waking up any dead people.

One night while nearly awakening the dead, a white man came from around the corner. Though no one other than Willie's mom had ever complained about the noise, we had an idea he wasn't too happy with all the noise we were making. We were playing a game called mother may I, which requires the players to stand a certain distance away from home or base and you call to the base or home asking permission to take steps closer. We were far away from base which required us to yell, "Mother may I take 10 steps", "10 steps, no you may not take 10 steps." As the man walked up to us I remember thinking either we woke up the dead or upset the living.

The man walked directly up to me with a polite smile on his face. He didn't say anything right away he just looked at us, then I noticed he began counting how many of us there were playing. Just as quickly as he appeared his turned and walked away. Not taking any chances we immediately went and sat on Willie's step. We were so quiet from that moment on when I whispered to Willie "what do you think he wanted", he must have said "what" 6 times before he could finally hear me. Not long after he left the man appeared again and this time he was walking fast right towards us. I thought maybe I should run home, because Willie could run in the house but I had several blocks to run to get home. As he walked up to us he began to speak. "I've been hearing you boys laugh for weeks now and sometimes it sounds so funny it makes me laugh too. I was at a baseball game in New York and began to laugh thinking about you, but I couldn't remember if there was 3 of you or 4 of you so I got 4 just to be safe." He then handed each one of us New York Yankees baseball caps and not cheap ones really nice ones. We were in such shock I don't think we were even able to say thank you. The man looked at us and say "Momma may I take 100 steps to go home" and then he started laughing even louder than we laughed earlier. We all laughed and he quietly went back around the corner.

We sat there just looking at these caps wondering why this man who had never spoken to us before decided to be so kind. He asked for nothing in return except for the 100 steps. I never saw him again, but this moment that we shared with him has been chiseled into not only my memory but my character and how I view people.

PRIDE

It is funny how history plays such a powerful role on the minds of tomorrow. I learned many things from reading Ebony magazine as a child. It was one of the only things I enjoyed reading because I saw black men and women who weren't out getting high or drunk. They were not just hanging on the corners or surrounding some card table to see who the neighborhood's best Checkers player was. These were black men and women who looked like me and they were actually doing things, and going places. I saw pictures of blacks in other countries and I saw my first pictures of Africa. I saw black elegant women and dark strong men. I wanted that to be me someday, it had to be me someday. The articles told of how blacks were treated and the things that we as blacks had to do in order to change things. The cartoon sketches had their hidden humor and if you paid attention you could catch why it was so funny, the drawing of the mailman creeping out the back door while the husband was coming in the front. I learned to tie my first necktie from an article in Ebony, well it wasn't really a tie, more like the belt from an old robe, but still I learned how to do it.

There was a great pride being black in Baltimore at that time and everyone seemed to be related to each other. You were either little brother, sista, cousin or some family member when you were greeted. You were immediately attached or associated and part of one collective community or village. Mr. Harold, Shawn and Devin's father was the only black man in the community that I knew of who was married to the mother of his children, polite to elders, and a positive role model. He always greeted me with a direct look; straight into my face as if he was some angel watching over the entire city. There are moments that will forever change the fabric of our lives and people who we seem to pattern ourselves after, even if, but for a moment. Mr. Harold was another person who would forever be a part of the man I am today. I never had an opportunity to tell him this, before he passed away or I was old enough to understand his impact on my life. To this day, I do not look at athletes, entertainers or reality stars as role models because they are not trained, hired or paid to model any specific behavior. I would dare to say that many of them may have been the bullies and class clowns that parents didn't want their kids to be like when they were young. Although the majority are actually stepping up and trying to do a good job, are they the people you wish your children to model themselves after? Many of these men in attempts to often escape their own traumatic histories or in need of treatments for their traumas and not able to provide effective mentoring to those now facing the same traumas in many cases.

Mr. Harold was a man who stood up, not with a multimillion dollar contract, not because he signed some contract that would be enough to feed his family generations after he was gone, but a man who stood up and filled the void, a man who looked into the eyes of the times that were and had heard the cry of a people calling out for their leaders to get up and he answered. "How are you doing today little brother?" he would ask me. I always stopped to think for a second before responding. Although my answer was always the same, I always had to think about it. It was like being in the presence of a King and he stopped to address you. I wanted to make certain that I gave him the level of respect he deserved. "I am good Mr. Harold, how are you today?" When he smiled it was like even if everything wasn't ok, it felt like they were going to somehow be ok. "You tell your mother I said hi and you be good." I responded, "Yes sir."

The majority of black men in south Baltimore during that time were either in jail, recently out of jail or nowhere to be found. Except for the men who would occasional drop by; the men in my community appeared to be lost and somewhat uncertain of their place. It appeared as if they had been part of some great battle and returned not necessarily defeated, but without purpose, hope or direction. Many had odd jobs in the box company or at Cross Street Market. Although they were men of color who were setting the path for us to later follow, we never saw them walking down our streets.

There were a few black men in South Baltimore in the late seventies and early eighties, who we referred to as Hobos or bums. These were people who were homeless, jobless and with little more than the money they were able to raise to purchase alcohol. Cheap, hard liquor such as Irish Rose, Mad Dog and in case you forgot, what's the word Thunderbird (a jingle sang about Thunderbird listed as one of the top 5 Bum wines) all consumed with the hopes of quickly chasing your troubles away. There was one man in particular whom I can honestly say, I never recall seeing sober. Each time I saw him he seemed to be intoxicated, ok well let's call it what it was, he was always drunk. But, the most memorable thing about him was that he always walked the streets of South Baltimore with a smile on his face and a song in his voice. It may or may not have been the liquor that made him this way, but I can still see the dirt on his face and hear him singing his song, "Every day is beautiful, to me." He was so tickled by his song that he didn't seem to notice the vicious words that were often yelled at him. Comments like, "Hey you dirty hobo!", "What are you smiling about?" or "Shut up and stop that singing!" made him continue to smile and walk on. Perhaps he didn't see his surroundings, but he only saw the beauty in knowing that God had given him another day to live and he celebrated each new day. I believe that, if the meek shall inherit the earth then his inheritance certainly would be immeasurable.

Near a wooded area south of Ostend Street bridge right next to what is now home to the Baltimore Raven's Football Stadium was an area that we called Hobo Jungle. It was considered a jungle because of how dense the trees were compared to the handful of trees throughout the rest of South Baltimore. Some houses had a single tree in front of them and a tree in the backyard, but for the most part, the only trees were located in Federal Hill Park and Hobo Jungle. Although the Hobos hung out in Hobo Jungle, it was a fascinating place with a stream, apple trees and plenty of rocks to skip across the water.

Only the bravest of the brave would ever consider venturing into Hobo Jungle and only with others who were equally as brave. Well they were brave until someone got scared and took off running. Then that same fear would prompt everyone to run and race to see who would get out first. I cannot remember a single time when one of these homeless men ever took the time to even notice we were there. They were often too busy trying to stay cool beneath a tree or bathing in the stream, but all it took was a leaf falling from a tree and the imagination of a child to get us off and running.

ANCHORS AWEIGH
One summer we found some barrels and wood in Hobo Jungle to explore. Back then there was no PlayStation 1, 2 or 3 and I don't think Atari 64 had even come on the market yet, so imagination sparked excitement and adventure. These barrels and wood were more than enough to trigger a battle or great adventure. The first thought we had was to build a fort, but who would we go to war with since few kids dared to enter Hobo Jungle. We decided to build a raft, that's it a raft and sail it to some other country. This was the creativity of children without thought of safety, physics, common sense, logic or supplies, but who needed any of that stuff when we had imagination.

So off we went rolling the barrels carrying the wood and someone found rope from an old clothes line. This was going to be such a great ship like military ships and pirate ships. We believed that even whales would quickly get out of the way of our ship. Since I was going to be the captain, the design had to be perfect. The barrels were placed at the bottom to keep the ship afloat while the wood was to provide a place for each of us to stand. The rope was originally supposed to hold the wood to the barrels, but I recalled an episode from Gilligan's Island where they made a raft and used rope and a sheet to create a sail. I knew not to even think about trying to take one of the few sheets we had outside the house for a sail regardless of how grand a ship we were trying to build. So I recruited Charlie, who was younger and always wanted to hang out with us. We agreed to let Charlie hang out with us if he did whatever we said. The things we made little Charlie do, I now look back and beg God for forgiveness, because we put him through hell. We would have him run into stores and grab candy then not even give him any or take things out of his house like the sheet that was destined to be the sail of our great ship.

In building our ship, we were prepared to do the impossible and I gave commands like, "Tie the ropes tight, get that wood straight and shiver me timbers." Even after serving in the United States Navy, I still don't have a clue what shiver me timbers means. I heard it in some black and white pirate movie and thought it sounded good. The other kids must have thought so too because they all laughed as we went on to build our ship. If my memory serves me correctly, it took all of three days to complete the project. My Project Management training I later received as an adult would have served us well back then, however the story would not be as humorous. The sun was bright and the wind seemed strong and blowing from the west, I knew this because it was coming from the direction of West Baltimore. It was time to cast off and I yelled, "Damn the torpedoes men, full speed ahead." We quickly looked around to make sure there were no adults who heard me cursing, then we were off.

You really have to be careful what you say around kids or allow them to hear. I would like to add at this point before going any further that God looks after fools and children.

Now back to the adventure. We were somehow able to get the rusted barrels, ok I know I left that out because someone may still try to ground me for this one. Alright so the barrels were rusted and the wood was a few sheets of plywood, but do not panic, I had a plan. We turned the barrels with holes up and marked the weak sections so everyone knew not to step there. Into the water our great ship went and each of the four of us stood proudly atop the deck like proud sailors headed out to sea. In about 40 seconds, wouldn't you know it, we must have been attacked by submarine torpedoes because we began to sink. Everyone jumped off and Charlie began to cry. I explained to him that I had to be the last one off the ship, even though I didn't know why, except I heard a captain must go down with his ship so I pushed him off before finally abandoning ship myself.

We never saw the attack coming nor did anyone get to see the sub that attacked us. As we made our way out of Hobo jungle all wet and tired from the adventure, we laughed and made accusations about who leaked our secret mission out and how they were able to find us so easily. We were already making plans on how we would be, "100 times more secret," and how we would bring bricks onboard to sink the enemy submarines the next time. I felt sad looking back at our sunken ship, but I promised myself I would avenge her.

It amazes me how often those who would judge others so quickly never get to truly see those whom they judge. The Hobos, drunks and bums that once roamed the streets of our community as a child would later make a vital impact on my future determination and success. I used them as examples to decide what I could not and was not going to be me. I was determined that whatever mistakes or bad decisions they had made, I was not going to repeat. The reactions children have to failures and problems, will later predict the way they handle them as adults. I never built another ship, but I learned a valuable lesson that day and every time I drive on the overpass section of interstate 95, I look down at what was once Hobo Jungle and remember our sunken ship.

Someday I will cross the lines of time, reach into infinity and take what's mine.

C. Montes 09/05/2007

The background of a painting takes up the majority of the painting; and this is where we find our heroes and villains, our victors and dried tears. Yet there are flowers that go unnoticed and with a single stroke of the artist brush, the true definition of his work is revealed. Sometimes we miss the people who stood in the background of the fabric of our lives helping to make us into the successful people we are today.

Hello Momma Unis. We haven't spoken in such a long time, but I think it is time I introduce you to those who never had the chance to meet you. I have known since your death that I would eventually have to address who you were and are to me and it is now time. In the Black communities in the 70's there were still a few black owned or operated businesses. One such business was May's Diner. It was around the corner from where we lived on West St. On the corner of Leadenhall and Cross Street, it was a Diner for blacks and Ms. May and her husband were the owners. There were so many characters who would come in and out of the diner. The diner sits buried in the background in the painting of my life. You might wonder how, as a young boy not old enough to cross the street alone, I ended up in the diner. Well, my mother's boyfriend Hamm as everyone called him knew Ms. May and her husband, who was a gate guard at a company called Grace. Hamm drove tractor trailers and would often have to go out of town.

The timeline places us back shortly after my being taken from my grandmother's home. It was never clear to me why they came to get me from the place I had always known as home to take me to a place where they had no time for me. When he had to travel out of town, my mother would go with him, so they paid Ms. May to keep me with her in her home and as she cared for me I would often end up with her in the diner. I would wonder around the diner and sometimes sit under the tables listening to adult conversations no child should have been permitted to hear or on occasion be allowed to help carry an item to a table where I would on occasion be given a tip. I would later begin to stay with Ms. Unis because things at the diner became too busy. Momma Unis as everyone knew·her, referred to me as her grandson and took very good care of me. She would insist each night that I say my prayers before climbing into bed and make sure on Sundays that I would go to church. Momma Unis hated when I had to go back and stay with my mother. Before I left her house, she would always make sure I had a meal and say, "If you need me remember I'm just around the corner." I had to be in the house or at least on the front steps by the time the street lights came on when I was with her. As evening fell, the buzzing sound was the lights beginning to power up and that signaled that I had about 60 seconds to get inside. You would see the young kids running as the lights began to buzz, as if these were alarm clocks. By the time I was 10 my mother and her boyfriend felt I was old enough to be at home alone so I was no longer sent to Momma Unis' home. When they were out of town I was free to do whatever I wanted, though I still feared Momma Unis seeing me on the street after the street lights came on.

My father's parents lived on Hanover Street, but my mother forbid me from seeing them, the only problem with that was I was me and as you've probably guessed I went to see them anyway. My father's mother was tall and proud, she seemed serious or perhaps concerned about the way I was being raised. I always thought of her as almost unreal because she seemed like one of the ladies in the Ebony magazines. My father's father was incredibly excited every time he would see me. He was a big man but somehow he seemed to come down to my size although I cannot recall what it was he did that made me feel that way. Once we were playing hide and go seek and I remember him hiding under the table with me. I thought this was so much fun until I remember he was supposed to be out looking for me while I was hiding. Perhaps my mother's anger with my father or her anger with her own parents made her fearful that they would take me away from her. One day someone told me that I needed to go to my grandparent's house. For some reason that time my mother was ok with me going. When I arrived there everyone seemed sad and the house appeared darker than normal. One of my aunts said that I needed to see my grandmother because it may be the last time I see her because she was dying. I remember looking in her eyes and feeling so afraid. I ran out of the house too afraid she would die while I was there. She passed away not long after that. I was told it was because she needed something done that her religious beliefs forbid her from doing. I learned many years later that not long after I left the house my father was brought there from jail to see his mother for the last time. I missed him by minutes. I have perhaps 3 at most memories of my father's mother, but her decision to place her religious belief before even her own life became the foundation of my own religious life. I wasn't allowed to attend her funeral because my mother thought my father would be there.

HUNGER

Many years later when driving in the car with my daughter who was 8 years old, she asked me after looking at some houses we passed by, why don't they clean up their front yards or fix up their houses. "You see baby", I said to her "not everyone has extra money to fix the outside of the home because some barely have enough to make sure the kids are eating inside the home." My memory went racing back to the little house on West Street. On the back of the house, there were rusted fences on the windows and the front of the brick house was painted red. As you entered the kitchen the refrigerator was more of a cooler for alcohol than storage for food and the cabinets held little more than false hopes. The walls were dirty and there was a smell of cigarettes and alcohol filling every bit of breathable air. That once familiar feeling of hunger for a moment returned to my stomach. Many may not understand the feeling when several days have passed and the only real food you have had to eat was served to you at school for lunch. The feeling of hunger that grips your stomach and seems to pull it all the way to your back. As we made our way up the street and my daughter seemed only further confused with the situation that had caused the people we were passing to live this way, I remembered my own mother spending her welfare check that she received around the 3rd of each month, by the 8th of each month. There would only be a small portion spent on groceries from the local grocery store chain Giant. I remember the bright lights and the fresh smells. Three decades later I still am a bit excited when shopping for groceries. My fridge always has extra as does the pantry now. I find myself sometimes opening the fridge with its bright LED lights or the door to the pantry to make certain there is food there and have been known to over stock them often perhaps because of a subconscious or even a conscious fear of ever being hungry again.

I remember clearly the feeling of hunger and the need for substance only to find empty cabinets and abandoned refrigerators. School lunches and summer programs were for some of us the only regular meals. On Saturdays the local church's summer programs did not have any functions, which meant no free boxed lunch. Back then Leadenhall St Baptist Church had a summer program for kids in the area and for kids like me it was the only balanced or certain meal we would sometimes receive during the summer. On this particular Saturday, it was a bit hot and as I opened the fridge door there was only a dim brown reflection coming from the half empty bottle of Johnny Walker. In the cabinets there were empty boxes that I fumbled through until I found some crackers in a box of Ritz crackers. It may not have seemed like much but the crackers were all I had to eat that day and I had to make them work. The kitchen was nearly always like this after the 15th of the month, when all the money and food stamps were gone. Whenever my mother's boyfriend brought food home, he would often take it directly to their bedroom, but on good days I was able to get what was remaining. Matthew 15:27 "Yes it is, Lord," she said. "Even the dogs eat the crumbs that fall from their master's table."

Survival depended mostly on the generosity of people whose houses I would frequent around dinner time. I never explained to aunts and friends why I was always there around dinner time. I managed to mix it up enough from house to house so as not to wear out my welcome at any one place. I was embarrassed as if it were my fault to be in this situation. When I would eat, I would never ask for seconds even though I was often still hungry. Someone later in life came to me and asked me, "Why don't you ever stop trying?" I asked them, if they had ever been hungry? I don't mean hungry because its 6pm and you normally eat by 5:30, but hungry because its Sunday and you haven't had a solid meal since Friday's lunch at school and the only guarantee is lunch Monday at school." After seeing the look on their face and realizing how emotional this made them, I backed off from the question shaking my head as the person answered, no nothing like that.

SUMMERTIME

There was always a part of the summer that was different, even better than the 3rd of the month. For a few weeks during the summer, I was allowed to go and stay with my Grand-mother Moma out in the country as we called it. Moma lived off of Ritchie Highway in Anne Arundel County, MD in a simple house with a wondrous garden in the rear. My plate was always the first plate to be made at Moma's house and unless I got up from the table or fell asleep while eating as I sometimes did, food was plentiful and seconds were always just given. The kitchen always smelled of food or seasoning from collard greens, cakes or snapped green beans from the garden. We would sit up the night before snapping green beans. Each day, my Grand-mother would take me to a store called Highs to get ice cream, cookies or some candy. One day when I was out in the garden exploring the many colors and kicking around dirt like so many little boys do, a snake suddenly appeared at my feet. I looked up towards the closed house door and as I opened my mouth to scream for help, there she was suddenly standing right there before me, my Grand-mother beating the snake into the ground. She beat that snake so bad I almost felt sorry for it. Quickly she lifted me into her arms looked me deep in my eyes and said words that erased every bit of the fear. She simply said, "Its ok baby, I got you. I'm here now" and that was the end of that conversation.

I remember a conversation between my mother and her own mother. The conversation seemed simple enough but I would later find that it carried an incredibly astonishing message within it.

My grand-mother (Moma) was cleaning her kitchen floor and my mother was standing in the kitchen with her waiting so she could take me back to her house. Moma had insisted that I eat before I leave and because the food was still cooking my mother would just have to wait. I do not recollect what triggered the conversation but Moma was explaining to my mother that the proper way to clean a floor was to get down on your hands and knees. My mother was quick to respond with, that was the old way of doing it and that was how only servants would clean floors now. She went on to explain that they have mops with handles so you would never have to get down on your knees again because that was the old way to do it. I sat in silence smelling the rolls baking in the oven and observed the exchange with the mind of a child who would one day be able to better grasp the true message and understanding of being a servant and falling to my knees. I was far too young to interpret Moma's response that day, but later in life when talking to God I was able to recognize how magnificent a response it was.

"Sometimes you have to fall down to your knees to finish the job."
~ Miley Glover (Moma)

Some might see the need in this message of humbling one's self, while others may see as my grand-mother would later add, how do you know it's clean if you never get down to look at it, but from an aspect of faith and hope I have watched many great men and women fall to their knees to get some job/mission complete or just to cry out for help when all hope seemed fleeing. I too have been found on my knees for reasons other than cleaning the floors littered by my hopes and dreams laying before me, like a servant crying to his master for deliverance.

A few years after this conversation when my Grand-mother died I wanted to crawl into the casket with her and just hold onto her. Being her oldest Grand-child I wanted to be strong but in that moment I felt all alone in the world. My hero was gone and the evil villains could now have their way. By this time the innocence of the young boy had been raped away by streets that had no mercy. I have heard many songs about the streets watching and the streets having your back, but the streets took a little boy and beat every bit of child out of him. When in the streets you gotta get dirty, so dirty I became. Fuck it, I became down right filthy. The innocence of a child was left lying in the gutter cold and hungry alongside broken bottles and trash that was once a bag holding weed and the bottles once held malt liquor. The drunken and drugged states were often a self-treated remedy for the traumatic experience often faced by those who saw their situations as dismal with little or no way of improvement. So rather than face the horror they would close their eyes and numb the pain. Summer had passed and so winter was coming.

WINTER

The number of drug arrest for adults between 1980 and 1990 more than doubled going from 500,000 in 1980 to over 1,000,000 in 1990 a report from the FBI Uniform Crime reports shows. With the absence of black men in the households higher than ever before, studies showing over 40% of black households in 1986 being headed by women and the disproportionate rate of blacks, victims and offenders of crimes in the 1980s. One study by the US department of Justice (Homicide Trends in the United States, 1980-2008) showing The victimization rate for blacks (27.8 Per 100,000) was 6 times higher than the rate for whites (4.5 per 100,000). The offending rate for blacks (34.4 per 100,000) was almost 8 times higher than the rate for whites (4.5 per 100,000) approximately a third (34%) of murder victims and almost half (49%) of the offenders were under age 25. For both victims and offenders, the rate per 100,000 peaked in the 18 to 24 year-old age group at 17.1 victims per 100,000 and 29.3 offenders per 100,000. And the Department of Health and Human Services has a study that shows between 1980 and 1990 the percentage of black homes with two parents in the household fell from just above 40% to just above 30%.

The state of black America showed little help and a hungry stomach gave little support to the notion that things would someday get better. I began finding ways to make certain I wouldn't go hungry. By now in the early 1980's my mother was sending me to get her weed with the money she received from the government to care for me (Welfare) and sometimes from the sale of her food stamps for cash. I had become so familiar with getting the drugs for her by then that I could tell the difference between a dime bag and a nickel bag once placed in my hand without even looking down at it.

Sometimes she would send me with as much as one hundred dollars to get her weed. Walking pass drug dealers and thieves, junkies and other criminals I had little to no time to be afraid because fear would get you robbed. There was one dealer she would send me to who when I would knock on his door I pretended to be especially brave looking him straight in his eye once telling him the bag was light. "What did you say boy?" "I said the bag is light and I aint paying for this is you don't have more I'll have to go somewhere else. By then only in the third or fourth grade he looked at me knowing I had one hundred dollars on me and me knowing he could have easily just knocked me down and taken it, he just laughed, "Ok Carl little man, my bad. I gave you the wrong bag." I locked my eyes on his hands making certain not to even blink or show any sign at all of fear. I took the new bag and walked away thinking how easily that could have gone the wrong way. Walking back from her dealer a police car pulled up next to me. I felt, what am I gonna do, they won't believe it's not my drugs. If I run he will certainly pursue me and if I don't he will stop me and find the drugs on me. "God please", I didn't even know what to ask God for I just cried out to him. The officer must have gotten a call because suddenly he just pulled away. That was my formal introduction into the game and by the time war was declared on drugs, like so many others I had already been a POW. I call it a formal introduction not because it was polite but only to show this was the actual acknowledged meeting between us two. The introduction was more like the hit from the group, Guns and Roses "Welcome to the jungle". The two lines that best described that moment were

"In the jungle, welcome to the jungle,
Watch it bring you to your knnn knne knees, knees
I want to watch you bleed

And

You know where you are?

You're down in the jungle baby, you're gonna dieee"

The song was from an album titled, "Appetite for Destruction" released in 1987.

FROM A BAD SITUATION TO TRAUMA

I would begin to skim some out of each bag and would sell what I took on my way back to the house. As I walked down the street thinking if I'm gonna get caught for carrying it I may as well get something for me out of it. At least this way I won't go hungry.

By the time I reached middle school I had already become quite familiar with which route the police patrolled and how to be invisible. Being invisible was a trait that I learned rather well and came to perfecting it as an art later in life with a silent walk. I knew when and which way to go, and after being jumped and beat up by four guys I would carry my mother's 45 automatic handgun to protect myself. The 45 automatic was one of the guns my mother and her boyfriend used to shoot at each other when I was younger that caused my mother to be arrested when one night he pulled his gun on her and she shot him, explaining simply "I told him, you pull that gun on me again you better be ready to use it." She only shot him in the leg and was soon released from jail. In school by this point of my life the teachers often would bore me because I became impatient with kids who took too long learning. They had the luxury of being stupid is how I saw it, however that was a luxury I could not yet afford. I would do things to help the boredom in school like learning to type in typing class with my hands crossed and writing short stories and poetry in middle school. I became even more concerned with math and sciences in school because I saw a more direct impact of these classes to my world. There were weights that had to be understood and calculating how long food would last from one date to another as well as understanding the exchange of money.

It amazes me that many would have been quick to label me with Attention-Deficit/Hyperactivity Disorder, stating that due to my lack of sustained attention, poor listening skills, poor organization, losing things and ease of distraction, but those who would do so would not take into account that the melodic rhythms hanging outside my window at night were not the sounds of wind chimes but the screams of sirens from police cars followed by the wailing of ambulances or the thunderous claps of guns shots. The qualifiers often for these labels often placed on children are not properly qualified.

When I took a job to sell cars later as a young man, they insisted that before I sell a car I get behind the wheel and drive the car. The importance of this experience would be so that I could understand what it was I would be working with and be able to qualify the vehicle to meet the customer's need. So to accurately diagnose or qualify these children, perhaps we need to go into their environment. Not in your cars, not from your heated and air conditioned offices, but walk where they have to walk. Walk past the man by the alley and notice how he stares at you and take note to the man standing next to him as he keeps looking around. The second man is trying to determine where the police may be and

CARL M. PRICE

who may witness what may happen next. Feel the cold stares run up and down your spine, the echoes of the screaming and when you run from the gunshots ringing out above your head be certain not to draw too much attention on yourself because then the shooter may aim at you. Tonight don't eat a full meal, eat a pack of noodles with ketchup followed with a tall glass of Kool-Aid with plenty of sugar. When you arrive at work tomorrow don't think about what happened to you the day before, pay attention only to those things going on at work now. Forget the fears you just had, ignore the lack of nutrients your body has had and now have a productive day.

I laugh when I hear people complain that they can't have a productive day if they forget a cup of coffee, yet we expect children to face daily traumatic experiences, lack of proper nutrition and little or no positive reinforcement, then arrive at school which may be the only place they can catch their breath and be completely focused in classrooms that are overcrowded led by instructors who are underpaid. The proper diagnosis many of these children may need to be given is Traumatic or Post Traumatic Stress Disorder. (Post-traumatic stress disorder, PTSD) is a severe anxiety disorder that can develop after exposure to any event that results in psychological trauma. This event may involve the threat of death to oneself or to someone else, or to one's own or someone else's physical, sexual, or psychological integrity, [1] overwhelming the individual's ability to cope Wikipedia.com.

CHILDREN IN WAR ENVIRONMENTS

Often when I heard of posttraumatic stress disorder I thought of veterans returning home from war. As I spoken with professionals across the country, I see more than ever that often what many children around the world, children orphaned in Africa by Aids, Russian children victim to the fall of governments, children in America and elsewhere introduced into the system after abuse, neglect, a combination of these or other issues is an experience that can only be properly defined as traumatic. At this point race loses its color, nationality loses it passport and what remains is those left with battle scars, both mental and at times physical. Like war veterans sometimes go on to lead very productive lives but some have no hope and seem lost with no one willing to fight for them.

Being sexually, physically or mentally abused is a tactic often used on prisoners of war referred to as torture. I would think it is necessary to mention at this point that torture under international law is prohibited. The United Nations has even formed a United Nations Convention Against Torture, yet there are over 500,000, half of a million children in America alone in Foster Care as a result of actions that can easily be qualified as torturous and countless others that have either left the system or not entered the system that are undergoing such experiences. Living as a refugee fleeing their birth home for safety in some foreign home, yet while these refugees are sheltered, fed and cared for most can never return home.

The traumatic experiences many children like myself had to face each day and many still face just walking home hoping to make it back alive is somehow not taken into consideration. Perhaps gun shots flying over ones head with sirens screeching all around you is not considered traumatic unless you are in a war. But this was a war and it was declared a war on October 14, 1982 by President Ronald Regan.

The commercials from the "War on Drugs", which was more of a War against solving the problems in the inner city. Problems of hopelessness and despair made it easy for drug dealers to tell kids in school, "Come on try it, all your friends are doing it."
War was declared on drugs but these organizations knew very little about the problem with drugs and decades later with countless lives lost both directly and indirectly to drugs, the battle plan is was not working.

SAFE ZONE
School was a safe zone for me, because there even the young drug

dealers could relax and be kids. They would often enjoy the chance to show off what they had purchased with their money from selling drugs like clean clothes, shoes or snacks. I was too busy coordinating my next move to be concerned with the show and tell of new shoes and clothes. I had to manage the two employees I had and come up with a way to branch out into other areas across town. By age 12, I had planned to have drug dealers who were not just children but mostly adults. My plan seemed ideal because they didn't have to be in school and could be working for me selling weed while I was in class.

When a teacher and principal approached me during class in the 7th grade for allegedly having a weapon in school I was already aware they would be coming. What they didn't know was the gun was not for school but for my extracurricular activities and protection when leaving school. I would often breathe a sigh of relief when I arrived at school because inside those walls was the only place I felt safe. I was so entertained when they so quietly searched my locker finding little more than a pack of cookies and a note with a smiley face. Into the classroom they came storming. As the gym teacher grabbed me, I suggested in a not so polite way that, he get his hands the "fuck off of me". He slapped me and as I looked to the teacher and the principle standing with him, I realized that neither would come to my aid so I stood to my feet and looked him in his eyes. He seemed frightened of what I might do to him. I walked out of the class down the hall and out of the school. Walking home I wondered, were they more upset that I challenged them or that I had done so and won by not getting caught. I was expelled from the school because no one would acknowledge I was hit by the gym teacher and it was said only that I was disruptive and stormed out. No one was willing to stand up for me so I learned to stand on my own.

ALLOW ME TO REINTRODUCE MYSELF
When I arrived at the new middle school, Diggs Johnson, I had to first meet with the Principal William H. Shaw. I remember noticing how he was dressed. He wore a suit and a tie and it all

seemed very well ironed and clean. When he spoke to me, he was very clear and his words demanded your attention. I recall thinking that this brother right here is more like what I'm talking about, he's smarter than the last ones. I immediately respected him and I finally saw someone who looked like me doing something positive. Then he made a statement that would forever shape my relationship with him and my life. He said, "I don't tolerate stupidity here and whatever craziness you were doing there I won't put up with it here." "Stupidity", I thought to myself with great alarm. Has he not seen my grades or scores, the IQ of this school may have just doubled with my entrance into the building?

Stupidity, the quality of being stupid and I were so far from each other we had never formally nor informally met. Was he not aware that I had successfully generated enough income part-time to finance my own small business and set up a franchise system surrounding real-estate (the drug corners) that Ray Kroc founder of McDonalds would have been impressed with himself? I ran my first hustle by the 2nd grade placing a single quarter in a newspaper stand then taking all the papers out and selling them. Talk about ROI (return on investment), I'm gonna have to show him and that became almost an obsession. I was more concerned about showing him how far from stupid I actually was than I was with providing for myself. Suddenly the drugs, the money and even my own hunger at times were now secondary.

Wikipedia.com defines self-awareness as the capacity for introspection and the ability to reconcile oneself as an individual separate from the environment and other individuals. This was my moment and I was self-aware

FINALLY

Finally a challenge worthy of my intellect. This man dared to use my name in the same sentence as the word stupid and I was determined to show him how wrong he was. I went after the smartest kids in the school and was determined to beat their scores, not just in one class but every class. I would stay after and do extra work just to show how much I knew and before long I was even helping out in the office. Occasionally, I would get in trouble in class because one of the teachers would bore me to the point where, I could no longer take it. I recall once screaming out, why should I be punished for his stupidity, if he doesn't get it (referring to one of the students who wasn't learning as quickly as the rest of the class) make him stay after or put him in another class but don't make the rest of us suffer because he doesn't get it and it was off to the office I was sent. I immediately regretted that outburst, that time not because I was sent to the office but because the student who wasn't getting it was my best friend.

I would always try anything I could to hurry and get out of the office before Mr. Shaw would see me. He one day pulled me into his office and asked what was I doing sitting in his office. I responded I did not know. He asked me, "Why would you do things if you don't know the reason you are doing them?" I didn't respond and he asked me "don't you hear me." I did hear him but was taking a moment to actually digest what it was he had said. He then said, "You are smarter than that." He in that moment had placed the responsibility of my destiny in my own hands.

It was like the scene from the movie Gladiator many years later, when Russell Crows screams out, "Is this not why you are here." The great gladiator was now in the coliseum with a formidable opponent, his destiny. "Were you not entertained, were you not entertained?" This is the moment where the theme song in a great action movie is queued up, this is where the sleeper is awakened. At that moment, I saw that I could control the path I would continue on and not be doomed to the environment or my surroundings.

After that, Mr. Shaw and I would frequently talk about math, history, great minds and being smart. I would hang around after school and help with anything I could. It didn't matter what it was, I learned to make copies and the filing system, I figured out how the intercom system worked and even helped some of the teachers. I became hungry for knowledge and he was a great chef serving some new plate of information each day. When I won awards, although my mother never showed up for the ceremonies, the secretaries in the office, assistant principal Ms. Dodd and Mr. Shaw always gave me that look like you better had won. Their response made me hold my head down and smile so no one could see how pleased I really was, like some great battle had just been won by a great warrior. I had even convinced them to let me play music over the intercom system for a few minutes before classes and make announcements to help get students pumped up and ready to learn and the other students loved it. It was like we had our own radio station for a few minutes each day with announcements and motivation to do well. The trauma of what we faced each day in our battlefield, the inner city of Baltimore was treated not with medication, but with caring and a call for us to be as good as we dared allow ourselves to be, a call to be great. Things were going great and then the question came, "What is wrong with your neck?" Mr. Shaw asked.

THEN CAME THE QUESTION

"What is wrong with your neck?" The left side of my neck had become very swollen. I responded "nothing", but he was very concerned. "I think you need to have that looked at", he said. After bringing it up with my mother, at first we were told it was simply a swollen gland. However as it continued to grow, her boyfriend became shockingly alarmed. I don't know if it was guilt for how he had treated me all those years or if it was after I explained to them that Mr. Shaw kept asking about it and I thought he may call home soon, if nothing was done.

Sitting in a bright colorful room at John Hopkins Hospital I remember being told that I had been diagnosed with nasopharyngeal carcinoma, Cancer. I didn't really understand what that meant because I had never broken a bone, had chicken pops, mumps or even a bad cold. I said okay, so give me the shot or bottle of pills and let me get out of here. My mother really didn't seem to look at me. I remembered hearing the word cancer before but I could not recall where I heard it, not yet recalling that my Grand-mother and grand-father had both died from cancer. For the first time, the look on my mother's face was that of fear and the very thought of her being afraid startled me. She didn't show this look even when she and her boyfriend sat in the living room shooting at each other and he ended up shot in the leg. So why was she afraid now and what could be so great that it would promote fear in her? Before that moment, I thought fear and her may have once met and once fear saw how she was, fear itself ran the other way, yet now fear was resting on her shoulder in victory.

When I returned to school and Mr. Shaw asked about the swelling on my neck, I simply explained "I have some type of cancer, going to the hospital in a few weeks to get something." His look should have told me that this was far more serious than I was understanding it to be, but I just went on with totaling up the numbers I was given to total. The secretaries began to look at me different as did Ms. Dodd. I didn't understand why until that first night. You see no one ever took the time to explain to me what it all meant nor what was about to happen to me, perhaps if they did, I may not have understood I was only 13. Then it began.

The beginning of the end? I remember being admitted and thinking, "why do I have to spend the night?" Later that evening when a nurse entered my room, she quickly explained that she had to give me an IV. Still not understanding what an IV was, Intravenous therapy, I simply smiled as she took my arm. After she cleaned an area on my arm, I saw the needle and every muscle in my adolescent body seemed to quickly become alarmed. I don't want to exaggerate but she stuck me and missed the veins so many times that another nurse came into the room after hearing me cry out. By the time Erin, the other nurse arrived in the room I was more than ready to just walk out. My arm was sore and bruised like that of a junkie with track marks up and down their arm. Erin took my arm and started rubbing it. She tilted her head to get my attention and said "its ok, I got it." She began to ask me questions like had I ever been to the hospital and how old I was, she joked about how tall I was and how she was even taller and then she said "ok got it." Got what I thought, then as I looked down I saw she had gotten the IV in not only on one try, but without me even being aware it had happened. I smiled as she wiped the tears from my eyes. As the fluid began to flow I thought to myself, big deal, they are just giving me water. It was hours later when Erin entered the room again, she explained to me I would feel something a little strange maybe as she changed the bags which were connected to the IV. Erin and I were the only ones in the room, my mother had gone home and suddenly I felt the chemo for the first time entering my veins. It was cold and hot at the same time and I could feel it as it slowly invaded each part of my body. First up my arm then down my chest. I remember looking at Erin thinking what is happening to me, "are you trying to kill me". It was a hard night, I went from cold shakes where they would cover me with heated blankets, to sweating like crazy. When I got up the next day to stretch my legs and saw all the other children on the unit who were being treated for cancer and leukemia, I suddenly had to know what was going on with me. Wasn't cancer a disease for old people, I thought.

Chapter 6

There Goes the Neighborhood

A social worker from the hospital visited the room and when I asked her what cancer was and what was wrong with me after handing me a few booklets to read she assured me not to worry there were 2 other boys who had the same type of cancer that I had. Devere and Andre would later stand as flags of hope for me though I never explained to them how much of an inspiration they were to me and my fight against cancer. Just knowing they had fought it, the same type I had and won gave me hope. Their cancers were caught much earlier than mine but they were still a sign of hope. Their victory against cancer would serve as my direction to recovery, as if a lighthouse in a great storm.

I remember reading very clearly what the booklet said about cancer and I can even remember the illustration. Cancer is when one abnormal cell attacks another normal cell causing it to become abnormal. As an adult in 2011, I recall watching the X-men first class movie and thinking when they explained what the mutants were, that's every child who has ever experienced cancer or leukemia, we were X-men. But as a child looking at the illustration of cancerous cells and the abrasive appearance while imagining these cells now inside my body attempting to kill me was not a movie, it was real and the only superpowers I would possess I later learned was my faith.

When most kids at the age of 13 are dealing with the normal changes in their bodies, like new hair, growing, deepened voices and puberty, I was lying in a bed being poked and prodded. I received so many x-rays, CAT scans and MRIs that I began to feel like I wasn't human anymore but a machine. They explained to me that I may lose all my teeth, go deaf, never be able to father children or go blind. "Wait, are you people trying to save me or kill me?" But wait there's more, you may lose your hair, have dizzy spells, find it hard to keep down food and in the end none of this may keep you alive.

I had just enough energy at the end of most days to take a deep breath and ask God "why me?" "Whatever I have done God please forgive me, because I am sorry," I cried out to God one night and I could actually feel his presence in the hospital room. Cancer had moved in and there went the neighborhood. I managed to stay in school in the beginning and if not for the staff at the school (Diggs Johnson) it would have been hell. Once the other kids found out that I had cancer, I became shunned and the stirs were so invasive that I only felt normal in the hospital. There was a girl I had a crush on since we were in elementary school together, when she saw me walking through the hall one day I couldn't help but notice she was looking at me. I smiled and became very excited, her eyes fixed on me seemed so welcoming and she seemed to smile as she said to another girl, "he is going to die". Although I've never been shot, it felt like I had just been shot point-blank in the chest. Even breathing seemed a bit more difficult as I walked down to the office and asked if I could go home because I was sick. Fighting back the tears from bursting into my eyes, I think they knew something else was wrong so they took me to the nurse's office. The school nurse looked at me and asked, "Are you ok?" I told her that I just wanted to leave. She asked if I would like to just stay in the office with her until my shuttle from the hospital arrived to take me in for radiation treatment. I waited there with her for the remaining hour. What no one at the school may have been aware of is that the first round of chemo didn't seem to go well because the tumor had actually gotten even bigger and things weren't going good.

I'M DYING

Johns Hopkins then had some of the best staff in the world. I asked the shuttle driver whose name was Rodney on our way to the hospital did he think I was going to die. Rodney laughed and I don't mean chuckled I mean he laughed out loud. My facial expression at that moment surely had to be one of shock because I could feel all the muscles in my face pulling up. Rodney responded, "Hey man we all gonna die, that's for certain, but I tell you this by the time they done with you in that hospital you may be the bionic man but you aint going nowhere anytime soon." As we passed through a traffic light we were both laughing. While lying in the machine getting my radiation treatment, I laughed again imagining the machine was actually making me a machine. The person administering the treatment heard me and stopped the machine then came running in thinking I was moaning in pain. When I explained to her that I was laughing because of something I heard earlier, she responded, "Don't do that, you scared the daylights out of me." That only made me laugh even more and I could hear her laughing as she walked out the room to start the machine again. She could not be in the room while the machine was running because of the radiation that the machine was producing, so there alone inside the room I laid trying not to laugh.

In its own way life was making me a machine. The increased absence of my mother from the hospital caused me to ask was my life worth sparing when so many kids who had what I saw as so much more to live for than me had passed away, robbed by cancer and leukemia. Amy was the first one that I knew who lost the battle. She was just one year older than me at the time and then Chris who wasn't even in middle school yet and saw me as his big brother. I was so afraid I would die any day that I stopped imagining anything further out than a few days.

Aside from the horrible smell that came with radiation and the complications I would later face as an adult due to the radiation the most difficult part of radiation was not the treatment but rather an experience in the waiting room. One day while waiting for my treatment sitting in the waiting room though on a warm day the waiting room seemed a bit colder than normal. An older gentleman sitting across from me waiting for his wife took a strange notice of me. It was not common for a child to be in that waiting room so I guess he felt the need to inquire why I was there. "You waiting for your grandparent" said the older gentleman. "No I'm here for my own treatment" I responded with the simple smile that children typically give to their elders out of respect. That was about all I could do because I had become so weak by then from the treatments. The man became nearly enraged throwing the magazine he had been reading onto the floor. I took my eyes away from the TV to stare at him, looking to my left from the corner of my eyes. "You should never joke like that" he said. After a very long day and the little energy I had, I really didn't feel the need to justify to a stranger why I was sitting in the waiting room of the radiation department at a hospital. His face turned three shades of red and the tension was obvious. When the big door opened followed by a nurse and she called my name and greeted me, I took the time to look back seeing the older man's face and the shame that now laid upon it. I'm not certain if it was guilt or shame or if he just felt sorry for me but all the color seemed to exit from his face. Although I understood that normally kids wouldn't be there, I was angry and hurt by this experience. Was my frail body not enough? Was my struggle just standing up not validation or qualification enough to be able to just sit and wait for what seemed like the continuous removal of my humanity?

At the end of that school year, I graduated from middle school. I was so skinny that the outfit I wore to the graduation was the smallest size the store had and it was still a bit too big for me. The last year of middle school was mostly with school work sent home because I had become too weak to come some days and other days were too risky with me having a low white blood cell count because of the chemo. I was determined to make it to graduation, if not just to show them I wasn't dead yet.

That summer I attended a camp in Virginia for kids with cancer and leukemia. Those of us from Baltimore rode in a shuttle to the National Institute of Health in Bethesda, MD where we met up with and got on buses which took us into the mountains of Front Royal, VA. Seeing all the kids who had parents in their lives and who came from what I assumed to be far greater financial backgrounds struggling with their battle I thought for sure I had no chance of surviving this cancer because I was alone and I was poor. Camp fantastic was a camp for kids with cancer and leukemia. The fresh air and being around other kids who were fighting the battle that I was fighting was extremely uplifting. I was no longer strange being so skinny and frail. It's funny how the kids at the camp who were white and black, all looked the same and the only differences we had was the cabin we slept in. One night we sat out looking at the stars and the sky had never seemed so beautiful to me. Andre looked at me and said with a smile full of certainty "you're gonna be okay man". Andre wasn't a doctor or a nurse, but he had gone through much of what I was going through and that alone validated his opinion to me.

I was quoted in The Washington Post in October 3, 1989 "I was very self-conscious and wouldn't even get my picture taken. But when I came here I didn't have to worry about how I looked." There are less than half a dozen pictures of me that were taken while I had cancer and each one was a picture of me at Camp Fantastic.

It wasn't long after that week away when I returned for further inpatient treatment. Although many cancer patients lose their hair because of the chemotherapy treatment, I still had a full head of hair and I had even begun to grow a few strands of hair on my face. I was changed to a different type of chemotherapy because the tumor was not yet going away.

REMOVING THE LAST OF MY HUMANITY

One night while lying on the hospital bed falling off to sleep I heard Erin enter my room carrying the bag with the new chemo.

As she switched the bags to begin my treatment she began to rub my arm where the chemo would enter my body. I didn't think much of it, I simply turned my head and closed my eyes. Within seconds a coldness began to attack my body. Beginning with my arm I could feel a great chill slowly working its way through my veins. Erin stepped out of the room and returned with warm heated blankets, but my body was still freezing, cold from the inside out. I could feel the chemotherapy entering every part of my body, this time like it was alive and searching for something. The look that I gave Erin must have frightened her because her response seemed just as frightened. Laying on my side I tucked my body in as tight as I could trying to store any heat that remained. There must have been four blankets covering me. To experience cold from the inside of your body out is a pain like none other. If I was becoming a machine this surely was the last step of removing my humanity, an attack that came from my own bloodstream. Chemo works by killing cancerous cells, the problem is chemo can't always tell the difference between cancerous cells and normal cells. One result of chemotherapy treatment can be low white blood cells.

By the second day of treatment the coldness was now bearable but I had barely enough energy to lift my hand. I was a teenage male at a point in my life when I should've been out running and climbing, but I didn't have enough energy to even sit up in bed. If there is one thing that cancer seems to always attack that would be pride. Because of the sudden lack of energy and my now immobility, I was unable to even make it to the bathroom. I tried with everything I had in me but I couldn't even sit up. Fortunately for me it was Erin who was on duty and when she walked into the room before I could explain to her that I couldn't make it to the bathroom she gave a gentle smile and helped me. It was the most humiliating moment of my life, two weeks later while eating dinner I noticed hair falling into my plate. Because of the chemotherapy I had begun to shed hair from my body. The hair on my head, eyebrows, eyelashes and finally the few strands of hair I had begun to grow on my face. I remember seeing many of the girls in the clinic who had lost their hair due to chemo wearing wigs and suddenly I felt very saddened. I thought how devastating it must be to be a girl, a teenage girl and to lose all your hair, but looking back now I can remember how beautiful every one of their eyes were. With the wigs or without the wigs their eyes seemed to be painted with brushstrokes from God. Brown eyes, blue eyes and even shades of green, their eyes told not there pain but of beauty even the cancer could not steal.

Later on I would begin receiving hyperthermia treatments. Hypothermia treatments expose the cancerous cells to high temperatures and kill those cells. They inserted a wire into my neck which went directly to the tumor and by then I even looked part android with this metal wire dangling from my neck. I remember joking with someone and explaining that they gave me the wire, so I could plug directly into their computers. By now I had attended another camp for kids with cancer and leukemia called Camp Sunrise located in Maryland. There was another kid there named Jimmy and we were junior counselors to some of the younger kids. We had a song we sang to get everyone laughing, it was the Hokey Pokey song. Jimmy was Hokey and I was Pokey and the kids seemed to love it. I don't think they loved it as much as we loved doing it and seeing the smiles on their faces. There was another kid at the hospital named Jason, who had had leukemia most of his life and now a teenager, he was an inspiration to many of us. Jason and his mother noticed that I was often alone in the hospital and they would stop by to see me. When Jason lost his battle to leukemia it was like losing a brother, perhaps like the feeling a soldier feels when a fellow soldier is killed in battle. It wasn't long after Jason's funeral before I would enter yet another new chapter in my life. But I would carry with me a part of Jason to honor him and his great battle.

While being treated for cancer I must have had hundreds to thousands of needles, dozens of X-rays, CAT scans and MRIs, I have had surgeries and specialist from ear nose and throat to hearing and the hardest thing to face was not the possibility of my own death, but the loss of friends in that battle.

Chapter 7

Foster Care

Facing the situation of being abruptly removed from what is often the only support and closest resemblance of love and family for children. Does the situation warrant a change in behavior away from what is normal and if so is such behavior justified? Is the acting out, running away and failure to respect authority at times the response to abnormal situations that have not been properly addressed? From home to home, family to family with no transitional training and a perceived expectation to simply adjust, should the child's behavior when unstable be considered abnormal even for this situation? For a great majority of those entering foster care, the experience of going into foster care and surviving foster care, yet surviving is just as traumatic if not in many cases more traumatic than what led them to needing to be in foster care. This often like the previous experience is a trauma left untreated. Often times the preferred treatment is medication, which does not treat the trauma but only treats the symptoms. It's like going to the doctor with a big lump growing out of your neck and explaining to the doctor you have a headache, the doctor gives you a prescription for the headache and sends you on your way. The big lump is never treated yet as long as you are medicated the headache goes away. A year later you discover you have had a tumor or cancer known as nasopharyngeal carcinoma and you may not make it, but at least you don't have those headaches any longer.

Prior to going into foster care my mother and her boyfriend argued a lot and I had to live with different family members on and off. I stayed with several aunt and even lived with my half-brother and his family. My brother though only a year older than me took his role as big brother seriously. One day I just didn't feel like going to anymore treatments and my brother threatened that if I didn't go again I would have to deal with him. I never referred to his mother by her name, I just called her mom and she referred to me as her other son.

My brother has two sisters with his mother and one of them and I loved to pick on each other. I would place clear wrap on the toilet seat or she would tap my cup while I was drinking to make me spill it. One night she waited for me to fall asleep and like a stealthy ninja she managed to paint my finger nails. When I woke up though I was furious I couldn't help but laugh. My brother's family wanted me to live with them but they were not permitted to keep me because they were not listed as family.

My introduction to foster care came with no preparation or even any set of expectations or explanations as to what I could expect or what was expected of me. The foster care worker whom I had very little interaction with from, only meeting this new stranger as he arrived at the hospital to take me to a foster (group) home. It was even strange for the hospital because he had never come there before, he had to should multiple forms of Identification as well as speak with his supervisor before the hospital would release me. The worker simply drove me and the green plastic trash bags containing all I owned in the world to a place I had no idea we would be going, down unfamiliar streets again into yet another foreign place, the only familiarity to what I had known was the new streets were painted with the many colors of broken glass poured into its gutters like some abstract piece of art depicting the many shattered dreams which laid there also. I felt as if I had wandered across Baltimore alone, not much unlike what I felt so many years before. I wasn't near my brother or any other family. The term Nomad quickly entered my vocabulary and I imagined myself like some nomadic tribesman wondering across the desserts of Africa. Upon entering the house, the introduction was limited to names and interrupted with the phrase and this will be your new home. How loosely the word home is added to conversation. There was no information given to me to explain why I was placed in this specific house or with this woman. I was never informed of her background or why she was even willing to have me in her house and so I wondered what she could have learned about me from a man who had known me for less than an hour.

It amazed me a few years ago when I was considering adopting a dog I was asked questions like where I lived and what my home was like and how big the back yard was to make certain the dog was being placed in a healthy environment, they suggested that I first spend some time with the dog prior to making such a big commitment, yet the first home I lived in or group facility rather than the term group home I was placed in with about 7 other teenage males had no yard but two alleys littered with trash and drug paraphernalia. Perhaps I thought to myself this is why dog adoptions and placements are more successful than those of children.

Forgive me if I just abruptly took you to another place in the story with no preparation or transitional period to introduce where we were headed, but this was the most effectual approach I could use to introduce you to what I had experienced like so many children entering foster care. I will now do for you what was never done for me and that is start over with the smoother approach taking into consideration how this may impact you and your understanding.

FOSTER 2.0

Dr. Small, my oncologist had become more of a close friend and big brother to me by this point after I had returned from Camp Fantastic. When he came into my hospital room, I could tell something was wrong. He looked at me and gave me that look, the same look he had given me right before telling me the tumor was not shrinking or that we would have to try some new chemo. When I asked him, "what's up?" he replied, "Nothing" but I knew something bad had to be on the way. I was so weakened from the Chemo that I barely had the strength to give it much thought.

The tumor was not shrinking, in fact, it seemed to be growing again and it was time to attempt something new. The hyperthermia treatments were suggested as an approach to now battle the tumor. He looked around the room seeing I was there alone he placed a form that needed to be signed over on the table. I reached over to sign the form and he asked what was I doing and explained that I was too young to sign the forms. "Who do you think has been signing the forms up to this point?" I asked him. He quickly left the room. In a weakened state from the chemo treatment I was receiving I was in and out. I became aware that the hospital room door had opened not much by the draft but by the sweet smell that seemed to suddenly lay itself upon the room. As I managed to pull together enough strength to turn to see where it had come from because it certainly wasn't coming from Dr. Small, I immediately noticed a uniformed officer at the door. I hadn't purchased any drugs for my mother in some time but I had been able to sneak out the hospital once or twice, IV bag in tow while I made my way downtown to get some fresh air without permission, but this officer was not from the hospital he was armed. It was instantly like the scene from one of the gangster movies I had seen all too often, I became afraid and worried. You see the flat foot, the coppers, the fuzz were here to put something on me, yeah that was it. Maybe they were here to frame me, it wasn't me I tell ya. They must have known I had done something but had no way of proving it so they were here to squeeze it out of me. So in the tradition of any great gangster scene and in the mind of a 13 year old child, I plotted my escape. I would rush pass the flat foot and bust out of here, cus there wasn't a hospital built that could hold me. There was a service elevator that not everyone knew of, I could take it down to the 2nd floor then hide in the Park building till the heat blew over, then make my get away.

Everyone knows that every gangster movie has a chase scene and my get away would be greater than any other. Forgetting I was weakened from the chemo as soon as I sat up preparing my great run I fell right back into the bed. That's when she came into the room. I'm not certain if the moment had anything to do with it, the meds I was on, puberty or my fascination with gangster movies but I'm telling you she was moving in slow motion, I mean everything seemed to suddenly slow down. In the movies this would be the scene where someone from the DA's (district attorneys) office would come in to make a deal. She was beautiful and the smell of sweetness she wore like a gown. I was so lost in the period of puberty, the chemo treatments and my weakness that I didn't have the slightest clue what she meant when she explained that she was from protective services. She said, I was being placed in foster care due to neglect because my mother had gotten into the pattern of just dropping me off at the hospital and leaving me to deal with the cancer and the treatments alone.

A case in California found that in the late 80s, 42% of children were placed in foster care because of neglect and 26% due to parent being absent or incapacitated.

It began with my mother bringing me to the hospital and spending a few hours in the room with me. After a few treatments, the hours shifted to minutes, and soon after the minutes shifted to just dropping me off at the door to the hospital. Her coping mechanism was to get hi and higher and even higher, numbing the pain of her only child dying. Self-treatment of trauma with drugs, a far more common practice than many would think. A few times while she was in the clinic with me you could smell the marijuana in her hair and on her clothing. I could tell others smelled it also because as they walked by they would look back as if in disbelief of what they had just smelled.

In the soup commercial that aired when I was young, a child had a cold and the mother sat by the child's side feeding him soup, adjusting his blanket and humming to him. I closed my eyes once while in the hospital and imagined that someone was there. I opened my eyes and looked at an empty chair and I could feel the very presence of God in the room. Throughout my life that feeling of his presence would forever be with me since then. I began to speak to God for the first time in my life. "What have I done to deserve this? If it's because I stole those newspapers I'm sorry. I only sold the drugs so that I could eat. Whatever have I done, I am sorry. I'm sorry" my voice sounding cracked because while going through the cancer my body was also going through changes from puberty causing my voice to change. It was like I could feel God crying while sitting in that chair. I then said to God, "just let me die. I have nothing to live for, I'll end up dead or in jail anyway so just let me die tonight". As I looked at the chair again, I knew God was with me and I could feel that somehow things were about to change. I remember falling asleep feeling okay knowing that I was not alone.

I was never told that I was going into foster care until a decision had already been made. The armed guard at my door was stationed there for fear that my mother's response would be violent, if she even showed up. The fear grew as she was notified that I was being taken and they moved me and hid me in another part of the hospital. Because I wasn't quite sure of the purpose of all this, I felt like I was betraying my mother and needed to demand to be returned home. However, the social worker's and nurses explained to me that I needed more help than my mother could provide. Hearing my mother arguing with staff as her voice echoed down the long hallway unaware how near I was, demanding my return caused me to question my loyalties and respect. The only thing I had known about foster care at that time was a television show called different strokes, where this wealthy white man took these two poor black boys as his sons.

Upon my arrival from the hospital to the group facility with my dark green plastic trash bag of clothing, I thought this is different from what I saw on TV. I referred to the placement as a facility not a home because it better fitted the definition of the word facility and not that of the word home.

> "Facility, to serve a specific function affording a convenience or service / Home, the place in which one's domestic affections are centered."

I would even say that the majority of the locations where children in foster care are placed are in fact not homes but instead facilities with the sole purpose of providing shelter, lodging, food and occasional transportation to the children placed there with little or no inclusion, support, motivation or treatment for previous traumas, but in the same sentence I must also add there are foster homes that do provide the children living in them with love, nurturing, development and healing. Many children in foster care feel that they are simply housed until they age out of the program, then they are dismissed into society with not as much as a good luck pat on the back. I still wonder why is it that neither the Department of Social Services nor the separate organizations that manage foster care have committees that seek feedback on how well the programs are working or grade the programs with members on these committees including those who are in these programs or were once in the programs (foster children). Often times those who have never experienced foster care dictate to those forced into foster care and regardless to the staggering numbers of failures ranging from the numbers of former foster youth ending up homeless, jobless or just passing from one system to another (foster care to welfare) these programs continue to pass on a psychology that has yet to include feedback from those it impacts.

In 2015 while standing at a gas station my eyes were drawn to a screen that asked, "How did you enjoy our service today?" I looked around thinking how odd and selected the middle number which then prompted a new screen asking, "What could we have done to make your visit better?" Two simple questions that if asked in a different situation could change the very practice of Foster Care today.

Tell me Carl, how did you enjoy how we serviced your situation?

Tell us Carl what could we have done to make this experience better?

THE SILENT WALK

Arriving at the group facility was a bit of a surprise because I had just left the hospital where I was being treated with chemotherapy. My energy level low, my white blood count down and the stress of entering foster care was a living nightmare. As we walked into the dimly lit hallway of the facility, a house that was an end unit row house, the foster care worker and I were guided into the living room. The foster care worker who I've known for less than an hour now simply introduced us and left. The lady whose house this was instructed me to take my bag upstairs to the room that I would share with two other boys. There was a total of seven foster children living in the home, all males in East Baltimore near Biddle Street. Shortly after arriving I was instructed to come downstairs to eat dinner. I looked at the lady untrusting and very nervously said, "I can't eat right now." She responded, "You better eat now because aint gonna be nothing later." Standing there watching the other boys inhale bologna sandwiches, I almost threw up just watching. Either she was not informed of my medical situation, didn't understand or didn't care. She insisted again that I eat. So I began to eat one of the bologna sandwiches, the kind with the red plastic around the outer edges of the bologna that when fried gets an air bubble in the center. It wasn't long before all I had eaten plus a little extra was vomited onto the floor. I was in the foster facility less than one week before the majority of the little bit of clothing that I had, had been stolen by the other boys.

The first night in foster care was the worse. Imagine laying in a bed that until just a few hours ago was not yours in a strange house with strange people you do not know. Laying in the bed it was impossible to force myself to fall asleep. Lights racing across the ceiling, chased by shadows, sounds echoing up the stairs met with smells and discomfort. My things sat in the corner in the green trash bag still unpacked. Who are these people, what is this place, why can't I just go live with my brother or back to my mother, I thought. Before I knew it I could see the sun coming up and I had gotten no sleep at all. By the time I made it downstairs I was tired with a major headache and the smells in the house accompanied by the loud TV and noise from outside seemed to be attempting to awaken the dead. I recall wishing they would have just left me alone where I was.

I couldn't sleep another night because I was used to getting up late and walking around the hospital to stretch my legs when I could, so I walked downstairs and as I arrived at the bottom of the stairs I could hear the lady speaking to her daughter. She explained how her daughter needed to get, "some of them kids", so she could "have some more money." I stood there still and very quiet, frightened what they would do if they knew I heard them. "This new one ain't gonna work out. I ain't got no time for no sick kids." As they began to move around, I could hear them beginning to make their way towards the stairs. I slowly lifted my foot paying close attention to how quickly I placed it on the stair and where I placed it so the stairs would not squeak. I was able to make it back to the room with them never knowing what I had learned. I would later learn that many kids in foster care also have learned this technique of quietly moving around so we could hear conversations, often those others in the houses would not care for us to be aware of. I would later call this the silent walk and as I explained to a group of kids in foster care many years later while speaking about trauma in foster care, they agreed this was a good name for it and how unanimously they had done the same silent walk at some point.

CAN ANYBODY HEAR ME?

When I returned to the hospital for additional treatment, I explained to the social worker that I would rather go back home to my mother than return to the group facility. I stated it was too much to deal with while fighting cancer. Trauma added to trauma can never lead to a healthy recovery. She suggested that I speak with the psychiatrist. I was forced to realize something while being treated for my own post-traumatic stress, something that would shape not only the way I approached life but how I would proceed through life. Like most children in Specialized Foster Care I had to see a counselor and like many, the counselor did nothing to help me. Questions like, "You seem quiet today, is something wrong? You don't seem to want to work well with others. Whenever you are here you don't seem interested, you never seem to be happy, have you tried looking at the positive?" and the same solution for every answer was medication. "You're quiet today, I think we should write a prescription to help you, you aren't getting along with your new foster parents perhaps we should write a prescription" and one day it came, "Carl you seem down are you sure you don't want to try some medication?"

That's it, I thought, enough! You wanna hear me talk well here goes. "My mother is a drug addict; my father went to jail when I was about 5 and I never really knew him; we were poor and the little money we got from welfare often went to supporting my mother's drug habit, when I finally get a little facial hair growing you know that puberty thing, I find out I have Cancer. Now since the previous chemo and radiation hasn't worked, they need to give me stronger chemo which will make me very sick, cause me to lose weight and pass out. The three hairs I had growing in above my lip are going to fall out along with the rest of the hair all over my body. I may end up deaf and lose all my teeth. Oh did I mention I'm a black kid growing up in Baltimore City where statistics already say I will possibly die of a violent death before I reach the age of 27. I'm in a group home because I was placed in foster care to help with this all, but I can't live in my brother's home with his family because you people say we aren't family enough. You think after all this I should be smiling and skipping around? Can I just have a moment of silence? When it hurts should I not feel pain, when all the world seems to have abandoned me? I was not even fully aware of what cancer was and all the many stereotypes that come along with being a foster child. When I want to cry, should I be laughing to make these meetings have some false pretense of success?"

The pen no longer moving, his focus on eye contact now broken and silence now rested upon the room. It's funny looking back now, I don't recall many sessions after that one. I also don't recall anyone telling me that there would no longer be sessions. While even then I understood the need to get me to talk was important, I felt that I need to be spoken with rather than at like I was unaware that my life was messed up or like I was somehow unable to comprehend the reality of what was happening.

The lesson that I took from that moment on was sometimes when it's raining, you have to see the rain even while you prepare for the sun's return, sometimes you must face the rain and feel what comes with the rain. At school it was hard enough smiling and appearing to have been living a normal life, coming home to people who seemed to have only an interest in the check they were receiving for you. I had no room or place to lodge a complaint and now this person who is said to be an expert's (the psychiatrist they had me see) only solution was to medicate me rather than help me see that although it is raining right now, the sun will surely rise again. What if he like so many others in my life believes that the sun would never rise again for me? If you seek to counsel someone, you are expected to guide them to a solution that would benefit them, not to place them in a state of pretense by dulling their senses. Teach me how to stand in the rain and I will learn to conquer the storms of life. Show me how to make it down the yellow brick road even when the lions, tigers and bears seem ready to pounce on me and I will find my way back home.

There was a group once called the Fugees, who on their album The Score had a song titled "The Mask"

"Put the mask upon the face just to make the next day,
Feds be hawkin me
Jokers be stalking me,

82

I walk the streets and camouflage my identity"

Often we attempt to mask our reality with some prescribed pretense of emotional stability which dulls the senses and cripples one's ability to deal with the storms that are certain to enter the roads we travel. Yes there are occasions where assistance through the use of medication may be required to help a person learn to deal with struggles and yes when appropriate this is a tool that should be used, however this should never be the first or only option. There should always be an attempt to help the person learn to deal with these situations rather than running behind the hand written prescriptions of lies that tell them everything is now ok because the drug has taken it all away like an old Calgon bath commercial from the 70s.

ALICE RUNNING AFTER THE RABBIT

Addictions to alcohol and drugs in many cases starts as a coping mechanism, dealing with stress, loneliness, lack of sleep and other situations which the temporary false disappearance of this situation gives a momentary relief from the situation and when the reality of the situation rebounds, often a feeling of or need to have the so be it temporary solution of drugs or alcohol becomes greater than the need of reality.

I watched how my mother would run to her clear plastic bags filled with weed and quickly roll a joint. As she would inhale her eyes would close as if turning from reality and when she exhaled it was as if she were allowed to see some false world which did not contain the problems of an abusive relationship, poverty or the hunger of a child. She would open her eyes and now have the half opened half closed sleepy (hi) eyes. Alice seemed to fall into her own wonderland. Her eyes would be partially open, you know that I'm high look, as if only seeing a partial reality of a world crumbling around her. Her tears were then allowed to turn into laughter and panic surrendered to peace while the storm raged in her life. As she awakened from this mirage one day, she found her only child dying from cancer, the same illness that had killed both her mother and father. She hears alarms screaming and the flashing lights of disaster all around her and so with the quickness of a rabbit she escapes back into the hole, leaving reality to fend for itself.

There was no way I ever wanted to go into this hole and there was no way anyone would make me go there. If it's raining, let me feel the rain, let it run down my face, allow me to hear the thunder, I wish to know what it is to fear the storm so I can learn to fight it. I can't fight it if I am not even aware it is there.

What do you think happens to someone who was given only medication to deal with problems? What about someone who was never taught how to deal with the storms that come with life or how to cope with and fix the problems?

The use of medications to deal with emotions and or trauma can lead to drug or alcohol addictions because like the ad when I was a child that was used for Morton's salt in everyone's life a little rain must fall. When children exit out of foster care, many of these addictions can be what leads to the alarming rate of foster care children who are drug addicts and or homeless.

According to several studies regarding runaways, more than one third had been in foster care a year before they took to the street and more than 1/5 who arrived at shelters came directly from foster or group home facilities. Now with no support, aide or place to call home these kids turn to drugs to yet again cover up the distress they are unable to face, the same type of distress that leads to the neglect of children who later end up in foster care.

How does Alice find her way back down the rabbit's hole? How do I deal with the flood I now have to face left over from the many rains left or ignored when I no longer have the means to obtain the prescribed drugs I once had? How can I get assistance from programs I am no longer eligible for? In many cases, this leads to self-medication via illegal and unmonitored self-treatment.

I wasn't given medication and I wasn't forced to return to the group facility after I explained that if they gave me medication, I would go out and sell it and if caught, I would say they had given me the medication with full knowledge that I intended to sell it. I was instead admitted and hospitalized for depression in a ward for people with eating disorders in the Johns Hopkins Meyer Building 4th floor. There I was facing multiple traumatic experiences now being housed with people who were suffering from eating disorders, that's right eating disorders. I would be forced to sit in group sessions and hear about why it was important for us to love ourselves and eat right. I would sit there thinking this was some wicked punishment for daring to have a voice that would cry out truth, a truth which no one wanted to or dared to hear.

During one of the session one of the patients said, "Well you're lucky, you're slim and you don't have the need to eat a lot." I remember looking at the person leading meeting and thinking, "are you kidding." I slim because I was sick and dying. I didn't eat a lot because anything I ate would come back up so I tried not to eat too much because the pain I felt when I would have to throw up because of the chemotherapy sessions. No one even knew I was in the hospital except the school and a few people in the hospital.

IN CARE OR IMPRISONED

One day Mr. Shaw came to the hospital to visit me. He was the only visitor I had had since Jason and his mom. Jason had become very ill but on his last visit to see me he and his mother brought me a bag full of goodies including candy bars, cookies and all kinds of good treats. After they dropped off the treats for me I went and sat in the open area and watched TV for about an hour and then went back to my room to grab a snack. I shared a room with a man who was being treated for bulimia. As I entered the room I found him sitting on the floor with empty wrappers all around him. Empty wrappers from all my snacks that were just brought there for me. All of them he had eaten and was now sitting on the floor in tears blaming me for having these things in the room. When I went to the staff and explained what he had done I was told I should have known not to have items like that in the ward.

I felt like I was being imprisoned, not because they feared I would hurt myself but because they feared I would speak up for myself. I had not yet heard of Nelson Mandela or become familiar with the term prisoner of war, but I had in fact become such a prisoner. I had dared to speak out against the bureaucracy that was foster care. When my visit with Mr. Shaw ended, I could see the sadness in his face. As he left, he kept looking back appearing to have something weighing heavily on his heart.

Eventually another foster care worker showed up explaining to me that they had found me a new home. Oh the words that they use when they dare to confuse a solution with little more than further retribution. This worker was excited and anxious. Around this time I was sent downstairs in the hospital to receive a CAT scan to see how my tumor was doing. Shortly after the CAT scan I was told I would need an MRI and after that a full body x-ray. Dr. Small called my room which wasn't uncommon because he checked up on me often. The uncommon thing was what he said next, "Your tumor is gone." I remember thinking what do you mean gone? For months I had been preparing to die, in fact sometimes I looked at death as a saving grace from the reality I faced. I struggled with going from dying to living, because in dying there was an eventual end to the pain, but God had other more important plans for me that I would later learn.

Anticipating another group facility, I was rather confused when they told me the foster family would be visiting me at the hospital. When they arrived they seemed like the perfect couple. The mother had a smile that seemed to light up the room, while the father with an accent from some island seemed kind and witty. I was told they had another foster child, a young boy named Jamal. When I arrived at their house a few days after their visit to the hospital Jamal and I hit it off right away. Things seemed to go smoothly until one day while the parents had stepped out and I was watching Jamal, his nose began to bleed. I thought nothing of it, but wanted to make them aware what was happening so I called them. Their first question was panicked and alarmed, "did you get any blood on you?" I responded I hadn't tried to help him yet, but was about to get some tissue for him. "Don't touch him," they demanded. I found this quite odd, but followed their instructions. When they arrived home they quickly took him into the bathroom like a triage with a box of rubber gloves and closed the door. The next day a foster care worker showed up and explained to me for the first time that Jamal had AIDS. I was furious thinking what would have happened if I had not called to alert them that his nose was bleeding and somehow his blood got into my system. I said to the worker "I just survived cancer and now you people almost caused me to get AIDS." He had nothing to say and seemed to care very little. There were no rules in place that required them to inform me just in case an incident were to occur. Jamal and I had become close like big brother little brother, so even when things became very tense with the foster father, I stayed there for Jamal feeling a need to protect him. One day the father threatened to punch me in the face and I had enough. I felt these people were receiving a monthly paycheck to care for me of which the absolute minimum was actually used towards me and here I was being threatened. I walked out of their house and went to a shopping center where I called the specialized foster care worker from a pay phone.

THERE'S NO PLACE LIKE HOME

After explaining the constant threats I told him I wanted to be moved out of that house. The rest of the conversation would echo in my head for the remainder of my life. His response was cold and emotionless he simply said, "Go home."

What is home to you? What is the difference between the four walls that make a house and a home? Stephanie Mills when she sang a song titled "Home", said
"When I think of home, I think of a place

Where there's love overflowing"

Home to me then was a place of safety, a place I could run to when all the world seemed against me and be at peace and welcomed. So I asked the worker, "when you go home, do you feel threatened, do you feel like you are no more than a means to get additional funding when you are at home?"

"Home to me is a place where I don't have to wonder if I'm welcomed, so you tell me where my home is and I'll go there. You tell me where is home?" Silence can be the loudest thing you ever hear sometimes and at that moment his silence screamed back at me that he was so ill prepared to handle this. For a cold second I feared what if they throw me back in the hospital so I then explained to him, we could go to court and speak to a judge about this, the judge being the judge that I had to see once a year to explain how I was doing in foster care, or they could get me out. This was where I decided my life was far too important to just allow it to blow in the wind and hope it all turned out ok. You see if God had decided I didn't get to die yet, I was going to have to do something with what he had given me.

You see though I didn't quite know about trauma or its impact I had become a regular at its table by now. I had a bottle of pills, and though I cannot recall the exact reason I had the pills I do recall that the pills were prescribed for me possibly pain pills from earlier and there was a warning that stated if accidentally taking 3 or more pills to contact your doctor immediately. The bottle seemed nearly full. After going into remission being placed in a group home, being admitted into a psychiatric ward with patients with eating disorders even though I had no type of eating disorder and the only reason I weighed so little at the time was because I was unable to keep down food due to the chemotherapy and now placed in a foster home where the foster father constantly threatens me, I found it amusing how no one up to this point ever bothered to ask me what I wanted, needed or how I felt about the decisions that were being made in my life. No one even bothered to consider if I even wanted to live any longer after facing a continuous stream of trauma. What is to be done when even the most basic needs such as physiological and safety found at the bottom of Maslow's hierarchy aren't even met? I looked at the bottle of pills I remember thinking that the child proof top being no restriction to me or the thoughts that now sat upon my mind served only as a reminder that the child I once was, was no longer. Silently, slowly and with precision I walked to the kitchen and to be sure not to draw attention to why I was in the kitchen of the split level home so late, I turned the faucet only enough to allow a light trickle of water to fall until the glass was filled. The lights remained off and into the dark hall I returned making my way to the bedroom door. As I sat on the bed because of my belief that suicide was an unforgivable sin I spoke with God in what I thought would be my last living thoughts.

God, I apologize for what I am about to do, you see I have nothing left, no more strength, hope or desire. This action will certainly cause me to end up in hell and I'm sure that I have now failed you, but I just have no energy left.

So I wouldn't chicken out I quickly opened the bottle dropping the white top to the floor and began taking all the pills. It took 3 handfuls and then the bottle was empty. I laid down noticing only the light coming through the window from outside and I thought I just wish God could somehow forgive me. I remember my eyes feeling too heavy to continue holding open and I could feel the coolness of the tears rolling down my face. My last thought was I'm sorry.

As you I'm sure have figured out I didn't die. I woke up with the warmth of the sun resting across my face like the feeling of a hand gently touching me. I thought I've really screwed up now, I tried to kill myself and couldn't even get that right now I may be brain dead or messed up my organs or was I dead and this was how death began. I attempted to lift my arm and it moved and then I sat up. I rushed into the bathroom and began testing different functions in front of the mirror. Yup you're still here I thought. So I began to speak to God again. Ok God. You don't seem to be interested in letting me leave so let's make an agreement. I will go through whatever you want me to but only if you go with me.

FAILING IS NO LONGER AN OPTION
I see this period in my life like the great battle of 1519 where Hernan Cortez orders his army to burn the boats they had used to travel to the battle in, thus leaving them only two choices, win or die. I decided failing would not be an option ever again in my life. If those who were responsible for my life would continue failing me, I would have to win this thing all alone. Because there wasn't a list of families waiting, I agreed to stay at the house a little longer at least until Jamal's condition which was by then was really bad got better or he passed away. A nurse began to stay at the house with Jamal and one night I was awakened by Jamal's cries for one of the foster parents to come into his room, but the cries went unanswered. A few hours later I was again awakened and told Jamal had passed away. Though we all must eventually die, there are those who when they leave us seem to take a little light from this place with them. I looked at the father thinking, you stand here now so impetuous, yet in his last breaths while he cried out to you, you didn't bother answering. The look I gave him was the last bit of communication I ever gave him. A few hours after Jamal's funeral when I buried my little brother, I moved from their house and with another family.

By now, I had lived in a group facility; admitted to live in a hospital; and with a family that seemed only interested in having children in their home for the money. Occasionally I would speak with Mr. Shaw even attending church sometimes with him and his wife. He was very serious about telling me to try hard and remain positive.

The next foster family I lived with was full of fun and laughter. We could sit up for hours just laughing. They encouraged me to go after my dreams. The only problem was that they were a young couple, who were still building their relationship with each other.

They were loving and kind and treated me like family rather than a check or part-time job, but what I needed at that time was healing from the trauma caused before entering foster care and the immeasurable amounts of trauma caused being in foster care. I was becoming a little stronger in recovering from cancer by then and had even grown my hair back, but now needed more than just a home. It was now time to begin treating the trauma. Part of the problem in the foster home I was in by then was not the home but there was nothing done to address the trauma caused by being admitted with people with eating disorders, the case worker, the failure to inform me that there was someone in the home who was HIV positive nor the threats from the foster father. I went into the next foster home with baggage from the last one and my life before that. I was unwilling and possibly unable to attach.

I was later given a new case worker who seemed not simply interested in me aging out so she could close my file by she was interested in what I wanted for me. She seemed to take an approach that none dared take before. I don't know if this was a new methodology or some last attempt but it was different.

WHERE IT ALL BEGAN TO CHANGE

We sat in the new case worker's car one day after a regular visit where she asked me to come outside with her for a minute. We sat there and talked about my doctors appointments and how I was feeling. We actually just talked. I didn't feel like I was being surveyed or examined, it was simply a conversation, then she asked me with her Alabama accent, "Well, what is it you want Carl?" The amazing thing was not that she asked but that she really wanted to know my answer. Her eyebrows raised and her posture leaning forward awaiting my response. She asked questions about school and college, she wanted to know what I was thinking and when the family I was then with became too much because they were not trained to help me deal with the trauma I had experienced, she asked me was there anyone who ever seemed to motivate me or who was always there. I explained I was a Nomad and I walked alone, all that I needed I carried with me, never fully unpacking and always ready to leave. I showed her a bag I always kept partially packed. Then she asked about the man who would always check on me, Mr. Shaw. That's not an option I explained he was my principal and he doesn't have time for a child. She suggested the idea to Mr. Shaw anyway. One day I was going to visit Mr. Shaw at the new school he was assigned to and I had taken the wrong bus. When I jumped off the bus hoping to get on another bus that would get me where I needed to be I thought I was already much later than I was supposed to be and had just given up. As the bus passed me and I looked across the street preparing to cross to take a bus back I heard a car horn and someone calling my name. It was Mr. Shaw and he had waited at the school as long as he could for me but had to leave by then. The timing was perfect because had I not caught the wrong bus and waited for the right one, we would have missed each other.

A few months after meeting Mr. Shaw near the bus stop, I arrived at the Shaw's house to live with them although there was opposition from many of the case workers. A child hears even when we may wish for them sometimes not to hear. I would hear other case workers explaining this was a bad idea and that I should not be allowed to move again. One was even noticed saying I did not deserve it. One night I became sick and was rushed to the emergency room. Watching how Mr. Shaw and his wife seemed far more concerned than me was like the sun rising on a cold morning giving both light and warmth. We grew on each other quickly. Mrs. Shaw, would become jealous that dad and I were always running around and insist that she and I got to spend time together as well. We would run and get subs, cheese steak subs with everything on them including onions or hit the mall. Mr. Shaw made certain I hadn't given up because all the trauma I had experienced. My new case worker was the first person to ever apologize for all the trauma caused since I entered foster care and that was needed.

Thoughts are energy and fear, happiness, laughter, sorrow and faith are thoughts. This being the case, a negative thought could then be considered to be negative energy and as we know a negative added to another negative increase the negative value pushing it further away from positive. Fear when added with sorrow and sometimes anxiety is negative upon negative upon negative and until a positive is introduced, it will remain negative. The addressing of the traumatic experiences I had faced were handled on a subconscious level because Mr. and Mrs. Shaw (my parents) and my case worker were aware and wanted me to have a chance at becoming whole again. I would need to repair the damage and so the introduction of positives began. Foster care for the most part up to that point (negative), Cancer (negative), Neglect, Abuse and poverty (all negative). Conversations were now about what I had been through and I was never judged for it, instead I was allowed to honestly express my feelings on what had happened which worked to restore the humanity that the trauma had stolen from me with positives.

The shame, pain and damage was addressed and then discussion on what would be next. Yes the trauma happened and now what. We began to implant new experiences, from the shows we would attend in New York, to the car trips deep into Virginia we became a family and by injecting new data, positive data into my subconscious mind my perspective began to change thus changing my conscious mind. By the time I was 15 I had started my own business, Air Raid Disc Jockeys. Often not even old enough to attend the parties I performed at as a disc jockey I was managing my own company.

One car trip heading south on Interstate 95, Mom's leg got a cramp in it and she asked dad to pull over, but because we were on the highway in traffic and traveling at 65 miles per hour he couldn't do it right away, so while still on the road with the car moving mom swung the door open to stretch her leg. "You better tell your daddy to pull this car over", she cried out. I laughed so hard tears were falling from my eyes. They both looked at me wondering why I was laughing. I was laughing because finally I had found the place where I felt safe a place where there was love overflowing and the traumatic experiences had been addressed thus placing them in my rear view mirror. The positives in my life were growing and now multiplying. We had so many great moments like that one, like mom trying to explain the birds and the bees to me on my way to college and me looking at dad laughing and him trying to keep a straight face or when I made it through basic training in the United States Navy and dad came in his full US Army Colonel uniform and made me solute him because he was a retired colonel and mom laughed at both of us. We didn't always agree and at times we didn't speak but they even to this day promote my growth, care for and cherish me while continuing to introduce positives.

YOU ARE NOW AT THE BEGINNING

There are those who may have read up to this point and now may not know what you should be feeling. You may feel sadness that a child had experienced such things, you may be confused at how any of this could have happened, some readers may not yet be able to understand what they are feeling and some may be smiling because of the end result. Whatever it is you are feeling, allow yourself to feel it and experience that feeling.

The summer after I graduated I began college for Computer Science, years later I enlisted in the United States where I struggled with only one area, running. I had to get a medical waiver just to be able to join because I was in remission from cancer and everyone thought I was surely crazy by then. I had passed every part of the US Navy's basic training program but could not pass the physical because I could not complete the required run.

With just a few days remaining before scheduled graduation after many had already dropped out of training I was told, "It's ok if you stop now Price. Everyone will understand that you had cancer. You can walk away saying you made it this far." I looked at the Petty Officer and said there would be no way I was going to quit. I asked to take the physical again and learned I only needed to pass the running part of the physical. I saw a familiar face at the facility who was going to be running and I knew he always finished and passed the run and though I was confused why he was there I was glad he was. I told him I would be running with him and as long as he kept running I would keep running. His name was Fitzgerald and he was from Washington D.C.

As we began to run I decided I would run until my legs fell off. The rules were you could not slow down to a walking pace and you had to finish in time. Time went on for what seemed like forever and it really began to feel like my legs were about to fall off. I was so tired, but Fitzgerald was still running and so was I. Suddenly I hear my name being called, no not called they were yelling, "PRICEEEEEEE. Get over here. The only called your name if you failed and when I walked up to the chief I explained that I hadn't slowed down and I was keeping up with Fitzgerald who never fails the running. The chief responded, "We know you didn't slow down, you finished over a lap ago and passed. We were waiting to see how far you would go." I had finished the race and kept running because I saw Fitzgerald still running, who I later learned wasn't there to pass the test, he was actually there trying to improve his already fast time. When I returned to tell my petty officer that I had passed he didn't say much, but on the day when we graduated he looked at me and smiled the smiling which screamed "I knew you could and would do it."

I would later end up with a medical discharge from the Navy because of complications from the cancer that I could not control, but I am proud to have served with honor, commitment and courage. I took from the Navy many lesson and I like to believe I arrived at basic training with many lesson already learned also.

Later in life I started other businesses, even sold some of them. I worked in corporate America for some incredible companies and one day I was watching the movie Annie with my daughter Hailey who by then was about 4 or 5. She asked me a question that would again change the path my life was taking. "Daddy, why doesn't she just live with her mommy and daddy?" I explained that sometimes kids are not able to live with their mommy or daddy because sometimes they need more than their mommy or daddy can provide. "It's like how Nanna and Pop Pop are my foster parents." You ever have one of those moments where you say something and then you realize you had planned to someday have that conversation just not at the moment you just did? Well this was one of those moments for me. You see I had never explained to Hailey that my parents, the people she knew as her grandparents were actually my foster parents. They had been there all her life including the day she was born.

As I explained to my daughter that I had been in foster care and had cancer, her little eyes looked up at me and just as I expected her to cry, she said "You need to go back and help them." When I left foster care I wanted nothing to ever do with it again so I didn't have any idea where to begin but I knew she was right. I reached out to a case worker that I knew from when I was in care because my last case worker had retired by then. I was asked if I would I be willing to speak to some people about some of what I had gone through and I agreed. A little later I was asked again would I be willing to speak to some people and I agreed before even asking who the people would be. I later found out it would be a United States Senate Hearing.

Since then I have traveled all over the country, working with different organizations, universities and families telling my story, the story of trauma to triumph, of how survival was never enough, how ordinary people in regular clothes are sometimes heroes and yes that happened to me now what. I have spoken before thousands and one on one because I know if not for the heroes in my life, my life would not be.

I made it out alive, but what have I become and at what cost? Often times when children enter foster care they enter it alone or with their siblings sometimes going with them. More often than not there is a disconnection from biological family because of the relocation and the disgrace that comes with the child entering foster care.

Why hadn't anyone come to help me or ever check to see how I was doing? Many years later, the severed relationships still remain damaged. Has my humanity returned or has the battle I have been forced to participate in caused further damage that now must be treated? No one from my family has ever asked what it was like, where I went or was it ok. It is a topic not discussed.

There is discussion within the foster child community on attachment disorder due to the trauma of being removed from families and in many cases living in multiple foster houses. These situations and experiences can cause an internal lack of trust in long term relationships or even a fear of the possibility of depending too much on people only to find yourself yet again alone. Having to be removed continuously from home to home and adjust to situations became the normal, but what has this cost me with my humanity or even my sanity? Have I become removed from the typical fears and sensitivities that I should have? Perhaps the answer is found when I hug my daughter who is 12 now. When I am holding her I never want to let her go. I tell her softly that I love her and how important she is to me and when she looks up at me I see in her eyes every bit of what humanity may have taken away from me is restored. In her eyes, I see hope that in her tomorrow a part of me gets to experience it all over again, the way it could have been and the way it should have been. When I'm talking with my son who is now 18 and he feels comfortable talking to me about anything that crosses his mind or when he comes to borrow one of my neck ties and he says I love you dad. When I mentor young kids in foster care or speak with foster parents and social workers, I am reminded that yes I made it out alive and I didn't just survive, I triumphed.

Chapter 8

Triumph

I have been asked many times when speaking on childhood trauma or foster care, what was done to make my experience successful and I can honestly say that it can be summed up in three steps.

ACKNOWLEDGE, TREAT AND DIRECT

First we must acknowledge the traumatic experiences that have caused the person to need assistance. Simply removing the person from the situation does not treat the trauma that now lays over them and is now embedded deep into their subconscious minds. Taking the approach of never speaking on the issue can never effectively lead to step two, treating the traumatic experiences. In all of these steps that were effective for me and I feel will be effective for others, it is important that those working with the child including within the community are trauma informed.

Trauma left untreated can lead to depression, social disconnection and an inability to succeed. The person's perspective must be addressed and changed. Please note that the word used here when working with perspective is changed not corrected. This is important to understand because perspective is neither correct nor incorrect. It is from the angle in which the person sees.

Attempting to treat trauma through the conscious mind is often met with little or no results. The memories while perhaps no longer in the conscious mind, remain in the subconscious mind and the subconscious mind's interpretations of positives and negatives shape the person's perspective on life and situations. I believe that the subconscious mind when left unaddressed will be left unchanged.

I would later have the successes in my life because my perception on every situation was if it doesn't kill me then, I still have time to win. Death being the only time I would not be able to add positives to offset or even replace the negatives. This perception came from the data planted into my subconscious mind by people like my parents William and Millie Shaw, my former case worker and the many others who insert positivity into my subconscious mind.

The final step is providing direction. If the only expectation the child has is stay in care until aging out at the age of 21 then that is the perceived only plan for the child and the child may assume that because this is the plan there are no other options. It is in no case safe to assume that the child is aware of all their possible options if all the options have not been presented to the child. A direction must be set up that is clear, attainable and buy in from the child must be present. This plan must have the ability to be adjusted when needed and when possible within comfort, the bar must be raised.

The plan should be adjustable in preparation for the possibility of changes that may arrive and the child's buy in will assist not only with support from the child, but may also assist in teaching him or her who to in the future create their own plans. Remember failing to plan is planning to fail.

Later in life as an adult I was able to reconnect with my biological mother. I learned that once I was in foster care she was able to find the strength to not only leave her abusive relationship, but also go to college. She later married a man who she loved and loved her dearly. I walked her down the aisle. I later buried her after she died from lung cancer.

My biological father and I had a long talk one day and now speak to each other regularly. As I have learned of his own traumas I am now just learning what his perspective of seeing your child dying, then going into foster care and disappearing for years must have been like and what about William and Millie Shaw, well mom doesn't swing the car door open any more but we are still family.

On December 10, 2009, President Barack Obama while receiving his Nobel Peace prize said, "We are not mere prisoners of fate." I stood to my feet in front of the television when I heard this because unknowingly my life has been a billboard for this very thought. I have been a witness to the notion that we are not locked into a set ending because of where we were born nor because of what has happened to us. I have been in the darkness, I have felt the pains and found the victory that for a time was impossible for me to see. It is important that I also add I am not the exception I am a possibility.

A MESSAGE

I sat in a room once with no lights on. As time went on the room became darker and darker as I did nothing to restore the light. Nothing was done to prevent the light, but nothing was done to deliver the light either. Eventually darkness consumed the room and light no longer appeared present. There in the darkness I discovered I had choices. I could either remain in the darkness or do something to introduce light. As I pondered this thought and began to notice how many times this has related to my life, I noticed in the distance though very faint, a red light. Startled for a moment I attempted to determine what caused this light to suddenly appear and now appear to only get brighter. Suddenly I realized that the red light was coming from the power switch on the surge protector under the TV stand. The interesting thing I began to consider is that the red light had been on the entire time, I just was not yet able to see it as my eyes were adjusting to the darkness. As I looked around I began to notice more light coming from different devices and shadows began to take shape. Doors began to be noticeable and I could now even see my own hands stretched out in front of me.

Often times when we are in the darkness the distant and faint lights of hope and possibility are not yet visible even though they are there. The adjustment can only fully take place if we leave our eyes open even in the darkness to eventually begin to see the light. We may have to turn our head and without any sense of direction at times reposition ourselves to find the light. I learned that day in my dark room as I have also learned in life that darkness is not always the absence of light but rather an inability sometimes to see the light.

So for those of you who cry and you don't know why but the tears seem to be pouring from your soul., the ones who can't seem to find your way, so life seems to feel as if it is simply spinning out of control, for those of you who feel so alone and so confused, know that your tears have the company of our tears. This storm that these tears form will clear the way and guide you home, just hold on. You are not alone and we are not mere prisoners of fate. You may have already taken your first step in finding your way home. You can make it, you must make it, and you will make it. If you are homeless, alone or thanking God that your experience wasn't so traumatic, you are not alone and you can still find your way home.

To those of you who work with children who have experienced trauma, thank you for being that hero that goes charging into the flames when everyone else appears to be running in the other direction. We know that all heroes don't wear tights under their clothing and for those of you sitting in your office with super hero tights on right now, well that's not a subject I'm able to help you with.

I was speaking at an event in 2015 with hundreds of attendees. Occasionally after I am done people who still have questions will wait to speak with me, after coming down from the stage and shaking hands while exchanging business cards a very kind woman asked if she could ask me a question. The woman was short and appeared to be older than me. After I nodded my head yes and leaned over to better hear her question she asked, "What do you think you will do if you ever reach your breaking point." For a moment it was like I could remember all the traumatic events at once and suddenly I laughed for a brief moment and then responded, "The same thing I've done each time I reached it before, take a deep breath and keep going".

FAQs (frequently asked questions)

What was it that made you keep going?

Though this is a question I have been asked by children in foster care, social workers, judges and countless others, it is always a question that is asked with hesitation. I am not certain if they fear the answer or if they fear the possibility of offending me for asking. I was introduced to religion at a very young age and faith has always in the hardest moments of my life been what I have fallen back to. As I have been moved into different homes as you can imagine I have been introduced to different views on religion and have never been asked what I believe. I have gone from Methodist, to Baptist, to Jehovah's Witness and Catholic yet the only thing I struggled with was if God actually heard me when I spoke to him.

What was the hardest part?

The hardest part was when my mother (Rosia) called and told me she had cancer. I went into a room closed the door and cried. This was my mother and I knew how hard not just physically but mentally this would be for her. She later died from the cancer and as I stood next to her body I could then understand all the trauma she herself had faced when I was a child from an abusive relationship with a man she was with for many years. I could see how she ran to the drugs and alcohol in an attempt to self-treat her own trauma.

What do you think now looking back?

I wish I could tell you that I look back and now see how easy it all really was, but that would not be true. When I look back at my life I see both the darkness and the light and I see it was not easy. I asked my brother just recently after nearly 30 years what it was like for him watching me go through all these things. He told me it was hard for him and how he cried about it all. I never thought of the pain those who loved me must have experienced.

What was the one thing that impacted you the most?

The thing that impacted me the most was the changing of my subconscious mind. I learned much later in life that it is the subconscious mind which controls the conscious mind. While my conscious mind was facing the struggle of fear, anxiety and countless other triggers, my subconscious mind saw the remote chance of hope and possibility.

How are you now?

If you have ever had the chance to hear me speak at an event or work with me you would see that I am a rather happy, motivated and passionate person. There is a saying about a ship is ok in the water as long as the ship doesn't allow the water to get in it.

ABOUT CARL M. PRICE

 As a motivational speaker, author, trainer and mentor, Carl M. Price has traveled the country speaking and training on childhood trauma, foster care, racial justice and motivating organizations and departments. He continuously assists multiple universities with training and serves on committees and boards, providing a voice and unique perspective.

With a bit of wit, humor and charm Carl has been able to shine light on the dark corners of trauma and show that with the proper support, winning can become not only a possibility, but an expectation.

AFFILIATIONS

- Advisory Committee Member for the Center for Child Welfare Trauma-informed Practice and Systems Change
- Baltimore Breakthrough Series Collaborative Faculty
- Therapeutic Foster Care Advisory Member

For more information about Carl M. Price, his projects, schedules or to book him for an engagement please visit our website at **www.carlmprice.com** or email **info@carlmprice.com**.

CARL M. PRICE

106